Preceding page: The elephant stables in the royal centre
Opposite: Detail of relief from the Hazara Rama temple
Following page: Octagonal watchtower in the *zenana* enclosure

DECCAN HERITAGE
FOUNDATION

Striving to promote and implement the preservation and
conservation of the historic monuments and cultural heritage
of the Deccan within a holistic environment and social context

Deccan Heritage Foundation Ltd
20-22 Bedford Row
London WC1R 4JS
www.deccanheritagefoundation.org

ISBN 978-81-8495-602-3
Fifth Jaico Impression 2019

© TEXT
John M Fritz & George Michell

© PHOTOGRAPHY
John Gollings

PRINTING
JAK Printers Pvt Ltd

PUBLISHED BY
JAICO PUBLISHING HOUSE
A-2, Jash Chambers, 7-A Sir Phirozshah Mehta Road,
Fort, Mumbai 400 001
jaicopub@jaicobooks.com
www.jaicobooks.com

Hampi Vijayanagara

HAMPI VIJAYANAGARA

John M Fritz & George Michell

PHOTOGRAPHY John Gollings

JAICO PUBLISHING HOUSE

Ahmedabad Bangalore Bhopal Bhubaneswar Chennai
Delhi Hyderabad Kolkata Lucknow Mumbai

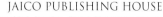

DECCAN HERITAGE
FOUNDATION

CONTENTS

Preface

Although modest in scope, this book is based on more than twenty seasons of fieldwork at Vijayanagara, the ruined medieval site that takes its name from the nearby village of Hampi. We have now hiked across most of Hampi's strikingly beautiful but rugged landscape, mapping all visible evidence of life here in the 14th, 15th and first half of the 16th centuries. But this does not mean that we have come to the end of our research. Many problems remain in understanding

Ruins of Beejanugg
The Rayels Elephant Stable
in Dec.' 1801.

the form and purpose of standing buildings, let alone the original appearance of the recently excavated structures, for which only the basement blocks survive. As for that part of Hampi's vast invisible archaeological heritage still buried beneath the ground, we can only resort to speculation. Yet of one thing we can be certain: if the archaeological heritage is preserved, there is sufficient work to occupy scholars for many years to come.

Given that we have reached the point in our investigation where we are still juggling our certainties and doubts, it comes as a welcome diversion to encapsulate our present understanding of the site in a condensed format intended for a general audience. Though we do not attempt to describe all the visible features of Vijayanagara, we have tried to include all the more important and accessible monuments.

Watercolour views made in 1799 by Indian artists in the service of Captain Colin Mackenzie: elephant stables (*left*), Lotus Mahal (*page 6*), and interior court of queens' bath (*page 7*)

INTRODUCING HAMPI

COMMONLY KNOWN AS HAMPI, the site of the imperial city of Vijayanagara is located on the Tungabhadra river in central Karnataka, near the border with Andhra Pradesh. Vijayanagara's fame derives from its role as capital of South India's largest, wealthiest and most powerful kingdom; hence its name, 'City of Victory'. Yet Hampi is not only of interest for its historical prestige and magnificent ruins; its remarkable landscape, religious associations and ongoing archaeological investigations make it an outstanding destination of international significance.

Granite landscape with the Tungabhadra river and Anjenadri hill in the distance

A MYTHICAL LANDSCAPE

For most visitors to Hampi, whether pilgrims or tourists, the first thing to be noticed is the remarkable scenery in this part of central Karnataka. Granite boulders of varying tones of grey, ochre and pink dominate the landscape, distributed either as hills and long ridges or as piles of rock that seem to have been thrown down by some primeval cataclysm. The terrain is, however, one of the most ancient and stable surfaces to be found anywhere on earth, its unique rocky appearance caused not by earthquake and upheaval, but by some three thousand million years of erosion, at first underground and then, when uplifted, by exposure to sun, wind and rain.

During this vast time-span the rock has weathered into spherical shapes, creating rounded and detached boulders, some of which are perched precariously, as if about to roll over. For centuries, this uniformly grained stone has provided an inexhaustible supply of building materials. Workmen fashioned blocks by cutting rows of closely spaced cubical holes into which they pounded wooden wedges; when wetted, the wood expanded, propagating deep cracks in the granite, the scars of which can still be seen.

The Tungabhadra river traverses the granite landscape in a northeasterly direction. Upstream, the river passes through a picturesque valley where large boulders frame cascades and rapids. By the time it reaches Hampi, it is forced into a narrow gorge hemmed in by granite peaks, the highest of which are Matanga hill on the south bank, rising 115 metres above the river, and Anjenadri hill a short distance from the north bank, almost 140 metres high. Flooding has worn away, polished and stained the rocks that border the river, and created islands, lagoons and small pools. A valley to the south of the river, running parallel to it in a southwest-northeast direction, marks another course of the river, probably an overflow in a wetter era. Yet further south, the granite outcrops gradually disappear and the landscape opens out

Marriage of Pampa and Virupaksha; ceiling painting from the Virupaksha temple complex

into a broad plain. This plain continues for more than 10 kilometres before ending at the foot of the steep slopes of the Sandur hills beyond the modern town of Hospet.

The fascination of Hampi's setting is by no means confined to its geology, for this is a mythical landscape imbued with the presence of gods, goddesses and heroes. The Tungabhadra and its surrounding pools and hills are linked with ancient legends described in the *sthalapurana*, a compendium of local myths associated with the Virupaksha temple at Hampi. This identifies the goddess Pampa with the village of Hampi, known in ancient times as Pampakshetra. Described as the 'mind-born' daughter of Brahma, the creator god, Pampa diligently performed penances on Hemakuta hill above the Tungabhadra river, thereby attracting the attention of Shiva. The god was seated in meditation nearby, having just destroyed Kama, the god of love, who had been sent to distract him. Shiva eventually betrothed himself to Pampa and married her, whereby she became identified with his consort Parvati, while he came to be known as 'Pampa's Lord', or Pampapati. He was also worshipped under the name of Virupaksha, literally 'he with oblique eyes'. Separate sanctuaries within the temple complex at Hampi accommodate images of both god and goddess, and numerous *linga* shrines affirm Shiva's association with Hemakuta hill. Pampa also gives her name to a pool known as Pampasarovar on the opposite bank of the Tungabhadra.

More important for the site as a whole, but probably not nearly as ancient, is its connection with the *Ramayana*. The Hampi region is identified as the forest domain of the monkeys, or Kishkindha, through which, in the Kannada and Telugu versions of the epic, the Pampa river flows. According to well-known episodes in the 'Kishkindha' chapter of the *Ramayana*, it is here that Rama and Lakshmana arrive in their quest for Rama's abducted wife, Sita. They encounter the monkey warrior Hanuman, who introduces them to his master, Sugriva, who had witnessed Sita being carried through the air by the demon Ravana. Hanuman also tells them about the struggle between Sugriva, the previous ruler of Kishkindha, and his impetuous brother Vali. Rama is persuaded to kill Vali and restore Sugriva to the throne. In return, Hanuman undertakes to search for Sita, eventually discovering her in captivity in Ravana's island fortress of Lanka. Hanuman returns to Kishkindha to inform Rama and Lakshmana of Sita's whereabouts and, after the monsoon season is over, they set out to rescue her.

Many of these events are identified with specific locations in the scenery around Hampi: Sugriva's cave close to the south bank of the Tungabhadra is believed to be where Sugriva hid the jewels dropped by Sita from Ravana's aerial chariot; the nearby pool, Sitasarovar, is named in her memory; Matanga hill is where Sugriva benefited from the magical protection of the sage Matanga who had placed a curse on Vali; the Kodandarama temple overlooking the Tungabhadra beneath Matanga hill marks the spot where Lakshmana crowned Sugriva after Vali was killed; Malyavanta hill is where Rama and Lakshmana waited during the monsoon. Such *Ramayana* references

Sugriva's cave consisting of a natural cleft in the granite boulders

Malyavanta hill with the *mandapas* and *gopura* of the Raghunatha temple on top

are complemented by relief images of Rama and Sita together with Lakshmana and Hanuman carved on to boulders in the landscape, some of which are incorporated into temples. Additional reliefs of Hanuman alone scattered around the site reiterate these links with the *Ramayana*.

Providing a date for these and other legendary associations is hardly possible, but there can be no doubt that human habitatation has existed in the area for at least 3,000 years. Prehistoric rock shelters abound in this part of

the Tungabhadra river valley, some with painted designs showing horsemen with spears and figures brandishing clubs, as well as lions, antelopes, horses and bulls. Examples of such paintings can be seen in the rocky overhangs in the hills west of the town of Anegondi on the northern bank of the Tungabhadra. Megalithic burial chambers with upright slabs laid on edge and capped with other large slabs are also found, such as those outside the village of Hiriye Benekal, about 12 kilometres to the west of Anegondi.

VIJAYANAGARA AND ITS RULERS

If Hampi's mythological dimensions appear to lie beyond the categories of historical time, the same cannot be said of Vijayanagara, the great city that was established here in the middle of the 14th century. It lasted until 1565 when it was sacked and subsequently deserted. Vijayanagara's history is relatively well known from inscriptions on contemporary monuments, travel accounts of foreign visitors to the empire, and chronicles of later Persian historians at the Deccan sultanate courts.

The foundation of Vijayanagara was a consequence of the invasions of southern India by the armies of the Delhi sultans at the beginning of the 14th century. Having vanquished the existing Hindu kingdoms of the region, the Delhi forces found themselves unable to hold on to their newly won lands. This created a power vacuum that offered opportunities for local chiefs to assert their autonomy, such as Sangama and his five sons. While the origin of the Sangamas is debatable, they were probably in the service of Kampila, the ruler of a minor kingdom in the Tungabhadra valley, when the Delhi forces arrived. Kampila valiantly resisted the conquerors, but was eventually killed in 1327. Soon after, two Sangama brothers,

Vijayanagara ruler worshipping at a *linga* shrine

Hukka, later known as Harihara I (1336-56), and Bukka (1356-77), established their legitimacy as leaders by patronizing the Virupaksha shrine at the Hampi *tirtha* on the south bank of the Tungabhadra and visiting the celebrated *matha* at Sringeri in the Western Ghats. They then raised a considerable army, including probably Muslim mercenaries, and set out to capture the territories lost to the Delhi invaders. So successful were Harihara and Bukka in this endeavour that within only a few decades they had brought the major part of South India under their control, including the distant lands of Tamil Nadu. Yet their efforts to extend their influence to the north of Hampi were largely unsuccessful because the sultans of the newly established Bahmani kingdom of the Deccan were pursuing a similarly ambitious policy of expansion.

Both Hukka and Bukka appear in the traditional foundation myth of the city, in which the two youthful chiefs are portrayed as hunting on the slopes of Matanga hill near Hampi, where they see a hare turn suddenly on their hounds. They consult Vidyaranya, their spiritual preceptor, who interprets this event as an auspicious sign indicating the favourable site for a new city. While it is by no means certain that Vidyaranya was an actual historical figure, there can be little doubt that Bukka was responsible for laying out the complex of ceremonial and residential structures that constituted the nucleus of a new capital, which he named Vijayanagara, City of Victory. Under Bukka's successor, Harihara II (1377-1404), this complex was contained within an extensive residential zone protected by a ring of massive fortification walls.

This period also saw the construction of various temples dedicated to Hindu deities as well as Jain *tirthankaras* (saints).

During the reigns of the later kings of the Sangama dynasty, notably Devaraya I (1406-22) and Devaraya II (1424-46), the Vijayanagara kingdom grew in size until it assumed the dimensions of an empire, extending from the Bay of Bengal on the east coast of southern India to the Arabian Sea on the west, and from the Krishna river in the north to the tip of Tamil Nadu in the south. The immense

Vijayanagara king making offerings to a priest; relief carving from the Hazara Rama temple wealth of this vast territory was diverted towards the city of Vijayanagara, which developed into an unrivalled showpiece of imperial splendour. Despite a marriage alliance between Devaraya I and Firuz Shah Bahmani, there was persistent conflict with the Bahmani kingdom to the north over control of the fertile lands at that lay between the Tungabhadra and Krishna rivers.

The later figures of the Sangama dynasty were less effective rulers and the fortunes of the empire declined as the 15th century progressed, with lands being lost to the Bahmanis, as well as to rebellious chiefs within the realm. Narasimha Saluva, who seized power in 1485, brought this situation to an end by restoring Vijayanagara's prestige and establishing a second dynasty at Vijayanagara. His reign lasted only until 1491, and there is little evidence of any building activity at the capital during this time. His successors proved incompetent and the situation once again deteriorated, with the government coming under the influence of officers of the Tuluva family who acted as regents. In 1505, Vira Narasimha Tuluva usurped the throne, signalling the rise to power of a third dynasty in Vijayanagara, and one that was able to sustain a line of successful rulers. Under Krishnadevaraya (1509-29) and his successor and half-brother, Achyutaraya (1529-42), the Vijayanagara empire

Portraits of a Vijayanagara king and queen; Archaeological Museum, Kamalapura

reached the climax of its power and extent. The capital was much expanded by the establishment of new religious complexes that formed the nuclei of distinct urban quarters. Some of these were located well away from the core walled zone of the city creating distinct suburban settlements.

Unfortunately, the Tuluva period was marred by repeated wars with the sultans to the north, particularly with the Adil Shahis of Bijapur who had succeeded to that portion of the former Bahmani state bordering on the Vijayanagara domains. Yet, Krishnadevaraya was able to attack Bijapur before embarking upon a military campaign to the Bay of Bengal coast in 1515-16, during which he raided the territories of the Gajapati kings of Orissa. He also made extended tours within his own domain, placating subordinate governors and worshipping conspicuously at important religious centres such as Tirupati (in Andhra Pradesh) and Chidambaram (in Tamil Nadu). Krishnadevaraya died while preparing to invade the territories of the Bijapur kingdom. On hearing of this news Achyutaraya had himself crowned in the temples at Tirupati and nearby Kalahasti, after which he too embarked on long expeditions. Achyutaraya also had to contend with the sultanates to the north, but under his able leadership, the prosperity of the empire and the wealth of its capital were sustained.

The last emperor of Vijayanagara, Sadashiva (1542-72), a nephew of Achyutaraya, had little opportunity to exercise power since the regent Ramaraya, son-in-law of Krishnadevaraya, assumed all government authority. As *de facto* ruler, Ramaraya effectively commanded the forces of the empire, but he antagonized the Deccan sultans to such an

Head of a Vijayanagara king or commander, Vitthala temple (*above*)
Destruction of the city; piles of overturned blocks and overgrown rubble in the royal centre (*right*)

extent that they formed a unique alliance against Vijayanagara. This led to the
catastrophic battle of January 1565, fought at a site near the village of
Talikota, about 100 kilometres north of the capital. The Vijayanagara army
was vanquished and after Ramaraya lost his life in combat, the city was
abandoned to enemy forces. Judging from the destruction of most of the
important buildings in the city, the conquering troops must have spent months
pillaging, looting and burning. So thorough was the devastation that it was
not possible for the later Vijayanagara rulers to re-establish their headquarters
there, despite several attempts. Eventually, they shifted to Penukonda and
then to Chandragiri, both in southern Andhra Pradesh, and finally to Velur in
Tamil Nadu. The fourth and last Vijayanagara dynasty, that of the Aravidus,
founded by a brother of Ramaraya, ruled over a steadily diminishing kingdom
for another hundred years, during which the former Vijayanagara capital
decayed further into ruins.

LAYOUT OF THE CAPITAL

Two hundred years of immense wealth and power are reflected in the plan of Vijayanagara, which is surely the largest for any contemporary city in India, with the central part alone measuring no less than 25 square kilometres. However, only those features built of solid masonry survive; notably the fortification walls and gateways, temples and shrines, colonnades and tanks, and ceremonial, recreational and residential structures associated with the king, court and military. These vestiges range from relatively complete buildings to piles of rubble lying on the ground, not to mention similar remains still buried beneath the earth. As for the houses and shops associated with the general population of the city, these have now vanished from view since they were built of impermanent materials such as mud, rubble, timber, thatch and terracotta tiles. In spite of this incomplete record, the overall plan of the capital and its different zones can still be determined.

A ring of massive fortification walls surrounds the central part of Vijayanagara, defining the urban core of the capital. Here is found the highest density of religious and secular buildings, as well as innumerable fragments of earthenware pottery. These data testify to a population that

Compound walls and watchtower in the royal centre of the city included Hindus, Jains and even Muslims of diverse social and economic backgrounds. Archaeological evidence suggests these varied populations lived in separate quarters with their own places of worship. These quarters were linked together by roads and paths. Information about these residential zones, however, is still far from complete, and archaeological exploration is still required.

The walls of the urban core create an approximately oval-shaped zone, greater than 4 kilometres along its southwest-northeast axis, with a temple complex on top of Malyavanta hill towards its eastern end. The perimeter walls run across granite ridges that are largely responsible for the irregular layout. Surviving gateways and alignments of shrines and other unidentified structures indicate a network of roads leading in radial fashion towards a

Hazara Rama temple surrounded by compounds of the royal centre

smaller walled zone positioned at the western end of the urban core. This is
the royal centre of the city, where the Vijayanagara emperor and much of his
court resided. Like the urban core within which it is contained, the royal
centre too was provided with a ring of defences delimiting an area almost 1.5
kilometres across, though this is no longer complete. The internal space of the
royal centre is divided into irregular walled compounds that seem to have
been functionally differentiated, some being set aside for public ceremonies,
others for more private and residential purposes. At the heart of the royal
centre stands the Hazara Rama temple, attributed to Devaraya I, which served
as a state chapel for the Vijayanagara emperor. Ceremonial halls and
platforms, stores and stables, as well as the palaces of the king's household
surround it. Many of the roads running through the urban core converge on
the open space in front of the Hazara Rama, further emphasizing the
significance of this temple within the overall planning of the city.

The royal centre spans the whole history of Vijayanagara. Inscriptions
near two gateways in the outer fortifications indicate that the walls outlining
its boundaries were already established by the middle of the 14th century.

The first stage of the multi-storeyed Mahanavami platform, intended for royal display, and the 'underground' temple dedicated to Virupaksha, the family deity of the royal family, are also assigned to the early Vijayanagara period. The Hazara Rama temple in the middle of the royal centre testifies to the substantial rebuilding of this zone in the first decades of the 15th century. The 16th-century additions to earlier structures confirm that the royal centre continued to be used up to the end of the Vijayanagara period.

To the north of the urban core is a 4-kilometre long valley defined by two parallel granite ridges running in a southwest-northeast direction. A stream running through the valley towards the Tungabhadra cuts through the remains of a large *bund* that once trapped water. On the south side of the valley is the Vijayanagara-period Turuttu canal that still feeds water to richly irrigated fields of sugarcane and banana. Given the overall absence of structural remains and associated pottery fragments, it seems likely that this valley was also used for agricultural purposes in Vijayanagara times.

This irrigated valley spatially segregates the urban core from the sacred centre of the city, which extends for about 2.5 kilometres along the south bank of the Tungabhadra. The sacred centre is divided into four independent quarters, or *puras*, each dominated by a walled temple complex:

The irrigated valley as seen from the steps climbing up to Matanga hill

Aerial view of the Tiruvengalanatha temple complex in the sacred centre

Hampi with its Virupaksha temple; Krishnapura with its Krishna temple; Achyutapura with its temple dedicated to Tiruvengalanatha; and Vitthalapura, taking its name from the Vitthala temple. Each of these nuclear shrines is approached along a colonnaded street, which served as a bazaar during festival times. Near each shrine is a large tank for bathing and religious ceremonies. The temples stand in high walled compounds surrounded by clusters of accessory shrines, colonnades, *mandapas*, wells, service buildings, and *chhatras*. The *puras* were linked by roads and pathways and marked by gateways, many still in use. Hampi is by far the oldest *pura* of the sacred centre, with shrines dating back to the 9th century, and remains an active religious quarter today. In contrast, the other three puras are mostly no older than the 16th century and have lost their original religious purpose; they are now reduced to archaeological zones devoid of any resident population.

While the urban core, royal centre and sacred centre are clearly the most important urban components of Vijayanagara, the city at its height spread well beyond these zones. The villages of Kamalapura, Malpannagudi and Anantashayanagudi, the small town of Anegondi, and the rapidly growing town of Hospet were all originally suburban settlements of the capital. At a distance of more than 25 kilometres from the urban core are the ruins of fort walls, gateways, canals, tanks, temples and Muslim tombs. These remains testify to a metropolitan region of more than 600 square kilometres, closely linked with the life of the capital.

PROTECTING & PROVISIONING THE CITY

Throughout their careers, the Vijayanagara emperors had to withstand repeated assaults from the armies of the sultanate kingdoms to the north as well as challenges from rival family members and rebellious governors within their own domains. Little wonder, then, that their capital was an immense stronghold. No doubt the choice of the Hampi region would have been dictated by its strategic advantages, since the Tungabhadra and the inhospitable rugged landscape cut off the site to the north. The concern of the earliest Vijayanagara kings with strengthening their capital may be seen in the fortifications of the royal centre and urban core laid out by Bukka and Harihara II. Both zones were ringed by walls, but only those that define the urban core are preserved complete. The defensive benefits of the rocky ridges were exploited wherever possible, with lines of straight walls running in

Fortification walls and watchtower in the eastern part of the urban core

between ranges to produce an irregular configuration of fortifications for the urban core. Fragmentary remains of a much larger sequence of concentric rings of ramparts fan out into the landscape beyond the urban core. However, the seven-gated fortresses mentioned by Abdul Razzaq, one of the first foreign visitors to Vijayanagara, can no longer be identified (*see page 122*).

All the surviving fortifications at Vijayanagara are built with massive earthworks encased on the outside by a layer of granite blocks laid one on top of another without any mortar, but with a slight incline. Additional strength is achieved by the use of square or rectangular bastions. The stone jointing is generally fine, but irregular, with the blocks touching each other only along their outer faces; structural stability is achieved mainly by massive earthen fill. This means that the walls look stronger than they are, and collapse easily when the earthen fill is displaced. Parapets on top of the fortifications, where preserved, consist of low walls or lines of slabs set on edge, sometimes with broad walkways suitable for soldiers. Better preserved are the remains of simple watchtowers from where guards surveyed the terrain. Foreign visitors noted that the fortifications were protected by moats, but these have been filled in, except for a portion beneath the walls near Kamalapura. Further protection from frontal attack was accomplished by fields of boulders set into

the ground, but these too have mostly vanished.

More solidly built than the walls, the city's stone gateways survive, even when the walls to either side have collapsed. The gateways follow a standard pattern: the entrance is flanked by massive bastions and roofed with flat slabs carried on lotus corbels, sometimes supporting an upper chamber and,

Bhima's gateway in the southern part of the urban core

in one example, a lofty dome on a quartet of pointed arches. Large wooden doors once abutted tall doorframes, occasionally with small passageways set into the walls to one side. The approaches to the more strategically important gateways are generally through projecting barbican enclosures that create bent entryways, preventing the enemy from riding straight through. Some of these barbicans are spacious enclosures with service structures and shrines housing protective gods.

The major roadways of the capital and even some of the pathways were paved in stone, as can be seen in those parts of the city where the dressed granite slabs or unmodified cobbles have not been robbed. Footpaths over the hills and ridges are marked by stairways constructed of slabs or cut into the face of rock, or by the worn sheen on granite surfaces caused by more than two centuries of continuous use.

In addition to protecting the capital, the Vijayanagara rulers also had to ensure a regular supply of water. Once again, the Hampi site proved advantageous for here the Tungabhadra flows through ridges and hills that offer opportunities for impounding and diverting its waters. (It is surely no accident that the modern Tungabhadra dam, the largest in Karnataka, is located only 15 kilometres southwest of Hampi.) As the river gradually lost elevation, *anicuts* (small dams) channelled water off into meandering canals and thence to tanks, fields and settlements. The ingenious use of the Tungabhadra to supply the capital with water made it possible for Vijayanagara to expand into a huge metropolis that could sustain several hundred thousand inhabitants. (The total population of the capital is still being debated.) The number would have increased considerably during festival times and war.

While the modern Tungabhadra dam and its supply channels and feeding basins have obliterated some of Vijayanagara's waterworks, portions of

Stone aqueduct conducting water through the royal centre

the city's original hydraulic system survive and are still in use. The tank just outside Kamalapura, for instance, fills up each year with monsoon rain, the water being trapped by its broad *bund* across which traffic now runs. This tank was the primary source of water for the royal centre, the water being conducted by means of masonry channels, elevated stone aqueducts and terracotta pipes to the ceremonial baths, pleasure pools and fountains in this zone. Tanks elsewhere in the city, including those associated with the major temple complexes, served as additional storage facilities for both the sacred centre and urban core. There were also numerous wells, many with access steps and platforms for hauling up the water.

Foreign visitors to the capital remarked on the profusion of orchards and gardens. Agriculture within the city walls naturally also depended on regular water supply, its primary source being canals fed by water diverted from the Tungabhadra. The most prominent working example of such a canal is the Hiriya kaluve, known today as the Turuttu or Turtha, that flows along the southern side of the irrigated valley and then continues in a southeastward direction through the urban core.

Extensive irrigated zones have also been identified outside the urban

core of Vijayanagara in the vast hinterland that surrounded the capital. Water was trapped by both small check dams as well as extensive ones, such as the Daroji reservoir more than 20 kilometres southeast of the urban core, where the massive *bund* is still plainly visible. National Highway 13 runs along the top of another *bund* to the south of Hospet, site of a large dam that seems never to have functioned properly. Thanks to these and other outlying waterworks, including masonry aqueducts, the mostly arid hinterland of the city was converted into richly irrigated fields of rice, pulses and other staple crops. Such productive

The Turuttu canal running through the irrigated valley.

outer zones maintained the permanent population of the city and made it possible for large numbers of troops and war animals to assemble here when the king and army were in residence.

All the foreign visitors remark upon the goods that filled the urban markets; according to the Portuguese Domingo Paes, Vijayanagara in the reign of Krishnadevaraya was "the best provided city in the world" (*see page 131*). However, the capital must not be considered as a natural trading centre but rather as an artificially created emporium sustained by courtly patronage, to which much of the wealth of the empire was diverted. Not only did the travellers marvel at the range of fresh meats, vegetables and fruits, presumably brought from the immediate hinterland of the capital, they were

Broken Chinese porcelains found in the royal centre (above). Irrigated fields outside the urban core (top).

also filled with wonder at the quantity of diamonds, emeralds and pearls for which Vijayanagara was famous. While Indian cloths of all types were available, sumptuous silks, brocades and velvets were also imported from Turkey, Persia and China. None these extravagances has been discovered in the excavations, but a few gold rings and chains and numerous fragments of imported Chinese porcelain dishes and bowls, most of them in the blue and white style of the 16th-century Ming period, have been found. All that remains today of the shops that stocked luxury goods are the empty colonnades of the temple bazaars and the buried streets of the urban core.

COURTLY LIFE

Contemporary sources, especially the chronicles of foreign visitors and the literary works of the period in Kannada and Telugu, make it clear that life at Vijayanagara focused on the king, his household and those in his immediate service. In this respect, Vijayanagara must be considered an artificial capital, dependent on the support of the royal figure; when this failed, as happened after the calamity of 1565, the city immediately ceased to exist. In reality, the king, court and military were hardly ever at Vijayanagara for prolonged periods, since they were compelled to be away for several months at a time, either touring their domain or conducting military campaigns into neighbouring hostile territories. However, life seems to have continued in the city, since the female and junior members of the royal family continued to reside there.

It is clear that the everyday routine of the Vijayanagara rulers was dominated by formal and ceremonial activities. The king spent many hours consulting with his ministers, commanders, spies and visitors, in the company of a private contingent of guards and attendants bearing flywhisks, standards and other regal insignia. On these occasions he dictated correspondence to secretaries who conveyed his orders to the palace staff, as well as to the viceroys and governors of distant imperial provinces. As the embodiment of *dharma* (moral duty), the king was required to sit in judgement on important disputes, or at least delegate a representative. Religious rites, too, had to be observed at different times of the day when the king was expected to worship the dynastically important divinities housed in the palace shrines. Meetings also took place with religious leaders and brahmin advisors from whom the Vijayanagara emperors often sought guidance.

It is still being argued to what extent the royal ministers, courtiers and advisors constituted a state bureaucracy, divided into departments that controlled the complex affairs of the Vijayanagara empire. The literary sources of the period emphasize the central symbolic role of the Vijayanagara king by

Courtly ceremonies and amusements; reliefs from the Mahanamavami platform

concentrating on the ceremonial aspects of government, especially formalized rites of reception and entertainment. Several structures uncovered by archaeologists in the royal centre confirm this ceremonial conception of the king's daily life: notably a spacious audience or judgement hall with 100 columns, a series of open courts suitable for grand assemblies, and a number of pools suitable for ritual bathing. The texts all agree that royal occasions involved exchanges of elaborate gifts and that one of the greatest honours for a courtier or visitor was to be invited to share betel with the king.

Nor were courtly amusements neglected in the royal routine. Contemporary texts delight in giving details of elaborate banquets with innumerable delicious dishes, entertainments with music and theatrical performances, and picnics and hunting expeditions on the outskirts of the city. Together with his courtiers, the king frequently enjoyed martial art displays, wrestling matches and animal fights. Beautiful maidens seem always to have

Loving couple and courtly women; panel from the Mahanavami platform

been present, and concubines frequently accompanied the king. The literary sources portray the Vijayanagara ruler surrounded by women who adore him and spoil him, and with whom he cannot resist flirting; in this respect, he is conceived as an irresistible erotic figure. Even when he leaves the palace, the king is rarely without the company of his favourites. The foreigners comment appreciatively on the dress, ornaments and varied accomplishments of these ladies, confirming that some were educated and talented courtesans.

However, the women who were seen with the king on these more public occasions are to be distinguished from the royal queens and female family members who were confined to segregated and strictly guarded zones within the palace. Female servants within the palaces attended the women and infant male relatives, who awaited visits from the king and the princes. The seclusion and privacy with which the courtly women were surrounded is corroborated by the surviving architecture of some parts of the royal centre, where residential structures can only be reached after following tortuous routes through multiple gateways, courts and corridors. Watchtowers rising above the palaces, looking out over the adjacent compounds and approach roads, provided additional security.

ARCHITECTURE AND ART

As the seat of imperial power, Vijayanagara was also a place of outstanding importance for architecture and the arts. The kings and their families, as well as their commanders and officers, not only erected buildings that bore their names, but also commissioned works of art, though none of these have survived the destruction of 1565. Since religious architecture was built of solid granite blocks laid without any mortar, it has survived to give a picture of the development of temple styles over a period of more than 200 years. The earliest Vijayanagara temples are the 14th-century shrines on Hemakuta hill. These elegant structures are built in a typical local idiom, comprising entrance porches with balcony seating, halls or *mandapas* with simple columns and double brackets, and shrines topped with pyramidal towers, all executed in granite. Temple architecture in the 15th century was expanded and elaborated, partly under the influence of the Tamil country incorporated into the Vijayanagara empire. The Hazara Rama temple in the middle of the royal centre is the finest example of this Tamil inspired idiom, as is evident from the finely worked decoration of its basement mouldings and pilastered walls. The brick and plaster tower over the sanctuary that rises in a succession of diminishing storeys also follows the Tamil tradition. The sanctuary is approached through a spacious *mandapa* with entrance porches on three sides.

14th-century shrine with three sanctuaries on Hemakuta hill

The climax of temple architecture at Vijayanagara occurred under the Tuluvas, beginning with Krishnadevaraya who added a magnificent *mandapa* to the Virupaksha temple complex at Hampi on the occasion of his coronation. He also built a multi-storeyed towered gateway, or *gopura* (replaced in later times), to serve as a monumental entrance to the newly renovated temple. Ultimately of Tamil origin, such spacious *mandapas* and lofty *gopuras* became hallmarks of the mature Vijayanagara style, to be repeated in all the later monuments of any magnitude at the capital, and reaching its artistic high point in the Vitthala temple complex. Like the other major complexes, the Vitthala is laid out in a linear sequence of *mandapas* leading to

the shrine of the divinity surrounded by a narrow unlit passageway. Associated goddesses and related deities are accommodated in smaller shrines standing freely within the walled compound of the temple.

These architectural developments were accompanied by a vibrant sculptural tradition, best seen in the mythological figures and narratives and the accessory maidens and guardians carved in relief onto granite columns, walls and ceilings. Highlights of Vijayanagara's sculptures include the reliefs on the Hazara Rama temple, where two entire cycles of *Ramayana* episodes are portrayed in stone, each episode of the story forming the subject of a separate composition. The royal reliefs on the outer compound walls of the same monument, portraying animals, soldiers and courtly women, are unique in South Indian art, as are the similarly royal subjects covering the granite sides of the nearby Mahanavami platform. Sculpture at Vijayanagara is also found on boulders scattered all over the site, either as relief compositions, such as *Ramayana* scenes or figures of Virabhadra and Hanuman as Anjaneya, or as gigantic three-dimensional monoliths of Ganesha or Narasimha. The technical virtuosity in the handling

16th-century *mandapa* extension of the Vitthala temple complex (*facing page*)
Krishna playing the flute; sculptural detail from the 15th-century Hazara Rama temple (*above*)

Vishnu and consorts with courtly attendants; plaster detail from the Hazara Rama temple

of the granite medium on this monumental scale is typical of Vijayanagara art.

Plaster sculptures also adorned the city's temples, as can be seen on sanctuary towers and *gopuras* where gods and goddesses are often flanked by courtly devotees. Similar plaster figures adorned the royal residences, but these are too fragmentary to be identified. Bronze icons must have been installed in temple sanctuaries, but not one example of the period survives at the site. (The brass images currently worshipped in the Virupaksha temple complex at Hampi are modern creations.)

Only the faintest indications of Vijayanagara period painting are seen in the temples, and no details can be made out, though surely they would have portrayed mythological topics. (The well-preserved paintings on the ceiling of Krishnadevaraya's *mandapa* in the Virupaksha temple date only from the 19th-century renovation.) Murals may also have graced the halls of the royal palaces, but these have completely vanished, together with the dyed and printed cottons, woven velvets and embroidered cloths, as well as the ivory thrones and beds, and gilded metallic thresholds, door frames and roof pinnacles.

No account of the architecture of Vijayanagara would be complete without taking note of structures within the royal centre, such as the Lotus Mahal and elephant stables, built in a distinctly Islamic manner. Inspired by contemporary architecture of the neighbouring Bahmani kingdom, these and other buildings in similar style have Islamic pointed arches, vaults and domes, and are decorated with cut plasterwork in stylized floral forms. This creative interaction with the Deccan artistic tradition should be considered as a manifestation of the cosmopolitan spirit of Vijayanagara courtly culture.

Religious cults

Hampi's mythical landscape gives visible expression to the religious cults that grew up at the site and which survive to the present day. As has already been pointed out, Hampi had been a riverside *tirtha* dedicated to the worship of Shiva, under the name Virupaksha, and a local goddess known as Pampa well before the establishment of Vijayanagara. In fact, evidence for the Virupaksha cult dates back to the 12th century, when this part of Karnataka came under the influence of the Virashaiva movement associated with Basasva, the celebrated social reformer. With the establishment of Vijayanagara, the cult gained an imperial dimension. The first Vijayanagara kings signed their documents engraved on copper plates with the words 'Shri Virupaksha', a practice that was continued by the later emperors at the capital. The importance of Virupaksha's support for the Vijayanagara rulers is borne out by the repeated benefactions to the temple complex at Hampi, as well as by the construction of a second smaller shrine to this deity within the confines of the royal centre intended for the private use of the king's household.

Ceremony in the open *mandapa* of the Virupaksha temple complex

Worship of the goddess Pampa in the Virupaksha temple complex

While the goddess Pampa seems to have been subordinated to Virupaksha as his consort, an inscription on the Hazara Rama temple in the royal centre specifies Pampa as the guardian goddess of Devaraya I, comparing her to other similar goddesses who protected several legendary kings. Nor was Pampa the only female divinity to be worshipped at the capital. Rock reliefs of bloodthirsty Kali are found at the site and a shrine consecrated to Kali under the name Ellamma faces on to the major road that once led into the royal centre from the northeast. The Ellamma shrine is still active, with periodic animal sacrifices and fire-walking ceremonies.

Another fierce deity who received worship in Vijayanagara times, and in fact continues to do so, was Shiva as Virabhadra. Images of Virabhadra are carved onto stone slabs set up at various points in the site, especially on hilltops and at gateways, indicating the protective nature of this warrior form of Shiva. By far the most impressive Virabhadra image is the 3.6-metre high sculpted slab within a gateway on the road leading south from Hampi, later converted into the Uddana Virabhadra temple.

The many spots referring to the *Ramayana* are sometimes marked by representations of the principal characters of the story sculpted in relief onto boulders. The Kodandarama temple, overlooking Chakratirtha on the Tungabhadra, and the Raghunatha temple, on the summit of Malyavanta hill, are both built around Ramayana rock carvings. Rama, Sita and Lakshmana were probably venerated in the Hazara Rama temple, but the stone or bronze images within the sanctuary have been lost. More numerous are the boulders, slabs and temple columns carved with Hanuman as Anjaneya, one arm raised in defiance, suggesting a popular cult of the *Ramayana* monkey hero. Such icons must have been considered as magically protective since, like those of Virabhadra, they are often positioned beside roadways and pathways.

All the cults noted so far may be considered indigenous, in that they formed an intrinsic part of Hampi's mythical landscape; significantly, they continue to flourish today. However, a number of other cults were introduced at Vijayanagara through courtly patronage, but these did not survive the destruction of the capital. They are linked with the Shrivaishnava movement founded by the south Indian saint Ramanuja in the 12th century, which gained great secular favour at Vijayanagara, particularly under the Tuluva emperors. The sanctuary of Venkateshvara, a popular Shrivaishnava deity at Tirumala near Tirupati, was developed into a major place of pilgrimage under Krishnadevaraya and Achyutaraya,

Relief carving of Hanuman as Anjaneya

both of whom donated votive portrait sculptures of themselves to this god. At Vijayanagara, at least eight shrines were built in honour of Venkateshvara, known in this part of Karnataka as Tiruvengalanatha. The largest such shrine, popularly known as Achyutaraya's temple, was founded by the king's brother-in-law and chief minister. The worship of Krishna also formed an important part of the Shrivaishnava cult and a temple dedicated to this divinity was erected by Krishnadevaraya to commemorate the success of the Vijayanagara army in Orissa. The stone image of the infant Krishna installed in the sanctuary of this newly-built temple was actually looted from the strategic fort of Udayagiri in Andhra Pradesh, which was taken on this military campaign. The veneration of Narasimha, the man-lion *avatara* of Vishnu, refers to the sanctuary of this god at Ahobilam, hidden away in the forested Eastern Ghats and patronized by many of the Telugu warrior chiefs employed by the Tuluvas. The link with these Telugu chiefs perhaps explains another of Krishnadevaraya's commissions, the awe-inspiring colossal monolith of Narasimha at Vijayanagara. Here, too, must be mentioned Vitthala, the aspect of Krishna associated with Pandharpur, the celebrated pilgrimage centre in southern Maharashtra. There exists a somewhat vague tradition that the

Head of monolithic Narasimha (*left*)
Sati stone showing a pillar with a hand, Nandi and a priest; to the rear of a shrine overlooking the Tungabhadra near Hampi (*left bottom*)

Vijayanagara monument was erected to house the Vitthala image rescued from Pandharpur at the time of the invasion of South India by the Delhi army, but the truth of this story has never been actually proven. Significantly, the three 16th-century *puras* of Vijayanagara's sacred centre – Krishna, Tiruvengalanatha and Vitthala – are all dedicated to these Shrivaishnava deities.

The cult of *alvars* also played an important role in the Shrivaishnava movement, as testified by the numerous shrines dedicated to these saintly preceptors at the capital. The Vitthala complex, in particular, is surrounded by shrines dedicated to Ramanuja, Tirumangai and other *alvars* that could be visited by devotees in an auspicious circuit.

The Jain *tirthankaras* also received worship at Vijayanagara, judging from the Jain shrines erected within the urban core and the outlying suburban quarters. Irugappa, one of Harihara II's generals, is an example of a Jain figure who attained importance at the Vijayanagara court. He built temples to the *tirthankaras* at Kamalapura and Anegondi.

Not all the cults practised in Vijayanagara times were focused on gods, goddesses and saints; ordinary humans also came to be worshipped, especially heroes killed in battle and their wives who committed *sati*. Scattered all over the site are memorial stones with relief carvings of the deceased that testify to the widespread reverence for such figures. Occasional inscriptions give the identity of the heroes or their wives, such as the example set into the ground behind a small temple overlooking the Tungabhadra, a short distance west of Hampi. (Several memorial stones are now displayed at the Archaeological Museum in Kamalapura.)

FESTIVALS

By far the most popular events at the capital were the great festivals that took place each year, many of them in the puras of the sacred centre. The chariot-pulling festivals at Hampi in Vijayanagara times, which commemorated both the betrothal and marriage of Virupaksha and Pampa, are still celebrated today. Busy fairs marked these auspicious occasions with all manner of items on sale in the bazaar street in front of the Virupaksha temple. Contemporary writers, such as Ahobala, the 16th-century author of the *Virupaksha Vasantosava Champu*, who describes a romantic assignation between a prince and a courtesan, confirm that there were huge crowds of visitors. Similar holidays with chariots and fairs were also observed in the Shrivaishnava complexes of the sacred centre, but none survives to the present day.

Courtiers celebrating the Vasantotsava festival; relief panel from the Mahanavami platform

Not all festivals at the capital were celebrated in and around the great religious monuments of the sacred centre; the royal centre was also a venue for holidays, such as the Vasantotsava, or spring festival. On this occasion, courtiers squirted each other with coloured water, much as in the present-day Holi festival that takes place during March-April. The Vijayanagara authors take delight in describing the king and the princes, accompanied by their queens and attendant maidens, all splashing each other in pools, sometimes continuing their antics in small boats. The popularity of the Vasantotsava with the Vijayanagara court may explain the numerous bathing ponds and water pavilions in the royal centre. Reliefs on monuments depict courtiers throwing

water at each other, as on the chloritic schist panels of the Mahanavami platform. Mock battles between Kama and his consort Rati, also associated with the Vasantotsava, are portrayed in relief, together with courtly maidens holding bows and arrows, beating drums and riding in boats.

It is, however, the Mahanavami that emerges as the greatest celebration at the capital because, on this occasion, the Vijayanagara emperor invited to the capital all his commanders, governors and subordinate officers. The Mahanavami took place in September-October, at the end of the wet season, an ideal moment to begin any military campaign. Indeed, the festival assumed a distinctly martial character since for nine days and nights the Vijayanagara king offered gifts and slaughtered animals to a divinity who, in turn, blessed the royal weapons and other regalia. The culmination of the Mahanavami was the tenth day, or Dasara, when the king reviewed processions of troops and animals.

While the Mahanavami may not have been a Vijayanagara invention, its rulers must be credited for developing the festival into a spectacular religious-political event. Mythologically, the Mahanavami was derived from the episode in the *Ramayana* where Rama propitiates Durga in order to win her support on the eve of the climactic battle with Ravana. Like Rama, the Vijayanagara king also worshipped Durga, so that he might also be imbued with sufficient force to govern his empire and overcome his enemies. Ideally, military expeditions were only embarked upon after the Mahanavami had been completed. In addition to its military significance, the festival was also of political importance because it was on this occasion that all subordinate chiefs declared their allegiance to the Vijayanagara emperor by paying tribute and pledging troops and animals.

In the end, however, the Mahanavami was a display of imperial magnificence intended to overwhelm visitors with the power and wealth of the Vijayanagara king; hence the processions of gorgeously caparisoned elephants and horses followed by maidens so laden with necklaces, armbands and anklets taken from the royal treasury that they had to be assisted by attendants. Musicians and drummers, bearers of flywhisks, banners and standards, and jesters and acrobats accompanied the royal animals and women. The climax of these celebrations was the great review that took place at some distance outside the city, where the king witnessed parades of troops and animals belonging to the different provincial governors and their commanders, after which he offered entertainment, sumptuous feasts and fireworks.

Processions of the Mahanavami festival on the compound walls of the Hazara Rama temple

MUSLIMS & EUROPEANS AT VIJAYANAGARA

Vijayanagara was not only the largest and wealthiest capital of its era in South India but by far the most cosmopolitan. Though frequently at war with the sultanate kingdoms to the north, there must have been a steady flow of

traffic between the two cultural zones. This explains the sultanate-influenced cavalry techniques that were employed to such good effect by the Vijayanagara army, the Persian style of the jackets and pointed caps worn by the kings, princes and ministers, and the sultanate inspired architecture of the pavilions, watchtowers and stables in the royal centre. That large numbers of Muslims, both Indian converts and immigrants from the Middle East and Central Asia, were employed by the Vijayanagara rulers is confirmed by the reports of foreign visitors and the presence at the capital of several Islamic quarters, complete with mosques and tombs.

Vijayanagara king receiving Muslim visitors (*top*)
Relief carvings from the Mahanavami platform: Central Asian Turkish dancers (*above*)

Devaraya II is renowned for keeping a copy of the Qur'an beside his throne so that he could take the oath of his Muslim officers. He often referred to himself as the 'sultan among Hindu kings', and so did many other Vijayanagara emperors.

It is, however, with horses that the Muslims at Vijayanagara are most often associated. The Vijayanagara kings were in constant need of a steady supply of horses, since the animals did not breed well in south India. Horses were required for the large cavalry companies that formed an essential part of the Vijayanagara military, but were also necessary for the king's personal use and private guard. More than elephants, it was the possession of horses that defined royal status in Vijayanagara times, which is why the emperors imported the finest animals from the Arabian peninsula. Throughout the 14th and 15th centuries, the transport of horses was undertaken by Arab merchants who commanded the Arabian Sea trade and who led the animals from the ports on the western coast, up through the forested Western Ghats to the capital. So concerned were the Vijayanagara kings to maintain a monopoly of these imported animals in competition with the Bahmanis, that they are supposed to have paid in gold for all horses that arrived in

Muslim tombs at Kadirampura

South India, including those that died on the journey.

Reliefs on the Mahanavami platform and Hazara Rama temple in the royal centre depict Central Asian Turks with characteristic pointed hats, long beards and flowing tunics. These foreigners are shown together with Arab horses in the role of grooms and trainers, rather than as riders and warriors. They are also portrayed as officers holding staffs, doorkeepers bearing weapons, drummers mounted on camels, dancers playing tambourines, and jesters. Such representations suggest that the 14th- and 15th-century Vijayanagara kings surrounded themselves with an inner circle of Turkish slaves who acted as officers, guards and entertainers, probably in imitation of the Delhi invaders of South India who also employed Turkish slaves for similar

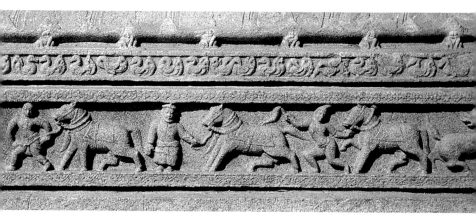

Horses with Portuguese trainers; panel from the Vitthala temple complex

purposes. This demonstrates yet another instance of cultural interaction
between Vijayanagara and the further Muslim world of the Middle East and
Central Asia.

Vijayanagara's fame spread to the Middle East. The city was visited in
1443 by Abdul Razzaq, an envoy of Shahrukh, the Timurid sultan who ruled
much of the Persian-speaking world from his capital in Herat. Razzaq's
chronicle is in the form of an official report, but his enthusiasm is apparent.
He was not the first foreigner to make the voyage to Vijayanagara. A few
years earlier, the Italian traveller Niccolò dei Conti was received by Devaraya
I. However, the Portuguese, the most important Europeans for Vijayanagara,
only arrived in the 16th century. Having established themselves in the port
of Goa, some 350 kilometres to the west, the Portuguese were able to capture
the Arabian Sea commerce from the Arabs and take control of the horse trade
with Vijayanagara. Temple reliefs of the period show horses being led by
figures wearing European-style hats, jackets and pantaloons.

The Portuguese maintained lively contacts with Vijayanagara
throughout the first half of the 16th century, with Goa benefiting enormously
from the business in horses and the commerce in diamonds and other
precious stones. Other than imported animals, the Vijayanagara emperors
may also have exploited European soldiers and firearms. Fernao Nuniz reports
that Portuguese musketeers assisted Krishnadevaraya when this emperor
successfully besieged the fort of Raichur in 1520. After Vijayanagara was
sacked and abandoned in 1565, the Portuguese lost their richest and best
paying client. Only then did they start to trade in earnest with the sultans of
Bijapur and the lesser rulers of South India.

INVESTIGATING HAMPI

Reduced to ruins and exposed to plunder, Vijayanagara was never able to recover its importance as a royal, military, cultural and trading centre. Worship in the Virupaksha temple at Hampi continued somehow during the 17th and 18th centuries, despite the turmoil caused by the struggles between the poligars (local chiefs), the *nizams* of Hyderabad, the Marathas, and Haidar Ali and Tipu Sultan of Mysore, all of whom laid claim to the Hampi region. With the last Anglo-Mysore war of 1799, the region passed into the hands of the British East India Company and some measure of stability was restored.

Less is known about the fate of the Vijayanagara site and its structures during this period. Evidence for the reuse of burned palaces and the construction of rubble buildings on top of earlier features indicate attempts to resettle the site, but by whom and when is not known. On the other hand, widespread vandalism is apparent. The floors of temple sanctuaries have been torn up, presumably by treasure seekers. While the destruction of the city's temples is usually attributed to the sack of 1565, the accounts recorded by 19th-century historians variously blame the soldiers of the Marathas and Haidar Ali.

Despite these vicissitudes, the former glory of Vijayanagara seems never to have been forgotten entirely. Indeed, it was one of the first historical sites in South India to attract the attention of the British amateur antiquarian Captain Colin Mackenzie, later to become Surveyor General of India. Mackenzie visited Hampi in December 1799, using Anegondi as his base. Describing the site as abandoned and inhabited by wild beasts, he and his team took refuge in the Virupaksha temple at Hampi since it was the only place that could be securely locked at night.

Apart from the occasional visits by other interested amateurs, it took about another 50 years before work at Vijayanagara was taken up in any systematic manner.

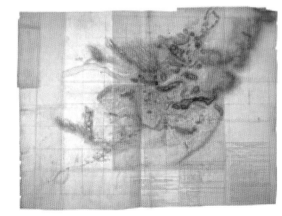

First map of Vijayanagara, 1799, by Colin Mackenzie (*see enlargement on pages 158-59*)

Print from a negative showing the octagonal pavilion, taken by Alexander Greenlaw in 1856

A key figure was Colonel Alexander Greenlaw who carried out a photographic documentation of the ruins in 1856. Using the newly developed callotype method of waxed-paper negatives, he took more than 60 views of the standing temples and courtly structures, the most exhaustive photographic coverage of any historical site in India up to that time. Greenlaw's magnificent photographs were never published, but were fortunately preserved in a private collection in England, to be rediscovered in the early 1980s. They show the monuments as they were before any conservation work was undertaken at the site, and so provide invaluable data for future reconstruction work.

It was almost another 30 years before Hampi benefited from serious scholarly attention. In 1885, Alexander Rea, head of the newly created Archaeological Survey of the Madras Presidency, surveyed the ruins and attempted to identify the different zones of the city and their principal monuments, following Abdul Razzaq's description of the city that had been published in translation only a few years earlier: hence the 'zenana' and the 'mint'. Epigraphical work was also taken up at this time and many inscriptions on the monuments at the site were copied, transcribed and translated until the turn of the 20th century when Robert Sewell brought out his path-breaking *A Forgotten Empire*. This book included a review of all known historical sources for Vijayanagara, accompanied by the first English translations of the descriptions of the capital by the two Portuguese visitors, Domingo Paes and Fernao Nuniz.

The early years of the 20th century witnessed a renewed enthusiasm for archaeology, with Vijayanagara being chosen as a site deserving particular attention. Under Rea and his successor, AH Longhurst, many monuments were cleared and repaired, and the labels that were assigned, such as 'elephant stables', 'guards' quarters' and 'Lotus Mahal', are still current. Knowledge about the site was deftly summarized in *Hampi Ruin, Described and Illustrated*, the guidebook brought out by Longhurst in 1925. With the construction of a road to Hampi and the conversion of a small temple at Kamalapura into an inspection bungalow, a visit to the site became possible for the first time.

After such promising beginnings, archaeological work at Hampi once again lapsed, with only the barest maintenance work being undertaken. This situation changed little once the Tungabhadra dam was completed in the early 1950s, though the resuscitation of the ancient canals and the construction of new water channels gradually led to the repopulating of the Hampi region. However helpful to farmers, the newly-established irrigation system caused considerable damage to the archaeological heritage by cutting through ancient features, obliterating whole suburbs, and encouraging destructive agricultural development. Meanwhile, the site continued to be ignored.

Interest in Vijayanagara seems to have gathered momentum during the 1970s, inspired partly by the excellent new guidebook on Hampi by D Devakunjari brought out by the Archaeological Survey of India, and reissued several times since. Two scholars, Pierre-Sylvain and Vasundhara Filliozat, began privately to examine inscriptions at the site, especially on the Vitthala temple, for which they also made measured drawings.

A significant advance as far as archaeological exploration is concerned was the decision taken in 1975 by the Indian government to initiate a national project at three medieval sites, including Hampi. As a result, both the Archaeological Survey and the Karnataka government's Department of Archaeology and Museums received funds to initiate extensive clearing and excavation work at the royal centre, tasks that have continued ever since,

Stepped tank in the royal centre discovered by the Archaeological Survey of India in the mid-1980s

with some interruptions. Among the most important discoveries made during these years has been a stepped tank of remarkable workmanship fashioned out of chloritic schist blocks and the basements of several residential structures, labelled as palaces by the excavators, one group of which has come to be known as the 'noblemen's quarter'.

An international team of archaeologists and architects has been working at the site since 1981, under the direction of John M Fritz and George Michell, as part of the Vijayanagara Research Project. Focusing on mapping and measuring the visible remains of the city, the project has concentrated on thoroughly documenting all standing buildings, architectural ruins and structural debris, as well as pottery and many types of modifications of granite bedrock and other indicators of past habitation wherever they occur. A related project, the Greater Metropolitan Survey, has expanded this documentation to encompass portions of the vast hinterland that surrounds the central core of the city.

Hampi under threat

In 1986, the Hampi group of monuments was inscribed on the UNESCO list of World Heritage sites and everything seemed set to bring to the site the international prestige and concerted protection that it so richly deserved. However, since then development has far outstripped the safeguarding of archaeological and cultural heritage. Until recently, increased prosperity and better transport meant that Hampi was overwhelmed each year with growing numbers of pilgrims and tourists. But in 2011, with little warning, Karnataka Government bulldozers began to demolish most of the private residences, hotels and restaurants in Hampi. In 2012 the campaign was extended to facilities that existed along the south bank of the river and even to guesthouses on the island opposite. This drastic action was contrary to UNESCO recommendations for World Heritage sites. As a result many inhabitants of the Hampi area became homeless and jobless refugees, and only a few places remained where visitors could buy supplies, eat or sleep. Now, while authorities attempt to shift tourism from "backpackers" to "five-star" visitors, neither group is adequately provided for. Meanwhile ashrams, guesthouses and even agricultural fields newly developed by temple authorities have been spared demolition. These institutions continue to enjoy patronage and income from devotees. But even here, clearance and building in the area has proceeded without documentation or conservation of the archaeological context.

Unfortunately, the site as a whole is also at risk. Quarrying of granite with drills and dynamite, and painting or cutting graffiti on boulders obviously damage the unique beauty of the landscape and adversely affect the archaeological integrity of the site. Meanwhile, the sinking of bore wells to extend cultivated land endangers the buried archaeological deposits. Neither the Archaeological Survey nor the Karnataka Government is equipped to control the central 25 square kilometres of the site, let alone the greater urban region. Hampi, in fact, demands to be considered in its entirety as an archaeological park, not merely as an assemblage of isolated monuments of historic significance, as is the case today. The Hampi World Heritage Area Management Authority, established in 2002, is in the process of implementing the Integrated Management Plan that has already been prepared. This will help safeguard the living, natural and archaeological heritage.

The efforts of the archaeologists at Hampi need also to be scrutinized, since so many monuments under their care are subjected to disfiguring repairs and surrounded by gardens that demand water pipes, storage towers and barbed-wire fences. The unfortunate experience of the Narasimha monolith, which was being renewed with the addition of modelled concrete features until work was halted by public outcry in the mid-1980s, only goes to show the gulf that exists between the archaeologists and conservationists. If Hampi is to be effectively preserved for future generations, then a complete change of attitude is required on the part of all the authorities, including government officials, archaeologists, temple committees, village leaders, agriculturists and tourist agencies. All must work in harmony to manage and preserve Vijayanagara's extraordinary cultural resources for future generations.

Bridge across the Tungabhadra constructed in the late 1990s before it collapsed unfinished into the river in January 2009. The debris has yet to be removed.

EXPLORING HAMPI

THE IMMENSITY OF VIJAYANAGARA, with all manner of ancient structures strewn about the rugged landscape, makes it impossible for visitors to tour the site in any straightforward manner. What follows here is an approximately circular itinerary that begins and ends at the Virupaksha complex at Hampi in the sacred centre of Vijayanagara, the only major temple at the site still in active worship. For those who have more time, the sights of Anegondi and other nearby villages are also included.

HAMPI & VIRUPAKSHA TEMPLE COMPLEX

As the principal destination for most visitors to Hampi, especially pilgrims coming from all over southern India and even parts of north India, the Virupaksha temple complex makes an obvious starting point for the itinerary described here. Hampi's population of about 1,500 is regularly augmented by huge crowds on festival occasions, most of whom come to worship Virupaksha and his two consorts, the goddesses Pampa and Bhuvaneshvari, in the main sanctuaries of the complex. Afterwards, pilgrims walk along the south bank of the Tungabhadra, visiting many of the spots associated with the

Ramayana. The village of Hampi clusters around a broad street that, until recently, functioned as a vivid and crowded bazaar, serving pilgrims and tourists much as it did in the past. Staring in the 1950s, when a rest-house, restaurants, shops and homes were built here, residential and commercial structures increasingly concealed the colonnades and shrines dating back to Vijayanagara times. Most of these additions have now been demolished by government authorities, leaving local people without places to live and work.

View of the Virupaksha temple complex and nearby Hemakuta hill with the Tungabhadra beyond

Hampi's bazaar is dominated at its western end by the imposing tower of the entrance *gopura* to the Virupaksha temple. Rising more than 50 metres above the street, the whitewashed tower gleams in the brilliant sunshine; at night it is brightly illuminated with electric lights. Yet, in spite of the religious and historical significance of the temple to which it serves as the principal

entrance, the present structure is of no great antiquity. Most of its granite basement and all of its painted brick and plaster tower date only from the beginning of the 19th century, when the monument, together with several structures in the bazaar street, were subject to extensive remodelling. Curiously, no historical information is available about the patron and builders responsible for these post-Vijayanagara period renovations.

In spite of its being a more recent structure, the *gopura* of the Virupaksha temple presents an imposing elevation, with the characteristic pyramidal tower divided into diminishing pilastered storeys and topped by a barrel-vaulted *shala* roof with gilded *kalasha* pinnacles. This scheme, which is typical of Vijayanagara-period *gopuras*, ultimately derives from Tamil prototypes of the 11th and 12th centuries. Passing through the lofty doorways of the interior passageway, visitors will note a massive pointed vault that is a clear sign of the more recent date of the gateway. The *gopura*

Entrance gopura of the Virupaksha temple at the end of the Hampi bazaar street

leads directly into a spacious rectangular court bounded by high walls. Straight ahead is a much smaller *gopura*. This is an authentic Vijayanagara period structure, being one of the additions made to the complex by Krishnadevaraya on the occasion of his coronation in 1510. Its granite lower portion, with a high basement and pilastered walls, and the somewhat squat, renovated brick and plaster pyramidal tower are characteristic of the 16th-century style. Another structure credited to Krishnadevaraya is the 100-columned hall occupying the left-hand rear (southwest) corner of the enclosure. Its spacious interior, arranged on three ascending levels, has an open hall in the middle bounded by columns

Krishnadevaraya's coronation mandapa in the Virupaksha temple complex

with cut-out colonettes, another typical 16th-century attribute. A small doorway in the side rear (south) wall leads to a kitchen through which runs a water channel cut into the rising bedrock that forms the floor of this colonnaded structure.

Since the other structures within the outer enclosure are of lesser interest, visitors should deposit their footwear at the small *gopura* just noted and move directly into the inner enclosure of the complex. This presents a more architecturally unified appearance because of the colonnades with cut-out colonettes lining the north and south sides, and the small Nandi pavilion, altars and *dipa-stambhas* (lamp columns) standing freely in the middle. The open *mandapa* of the main temple occupies the western end of the enclosure. An inscription on a slab by the side of the entrance steps states that

VIRUPAKSHA TEMPLE COMPLEX

A   Main shrine
B   Mandapa extension with painted ceiling
C   Pampadevi and Bhuvaneshvari shrines
D   Manmatha tank
E   100-columned hall
F   Kitchen
G   Gopura

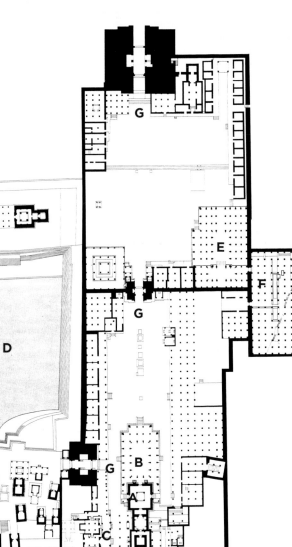

Krishnadevaraya built this *mandapa* in 1510; indeed, the contribution of this royal patron is evident in the striking originality of its architecture and carved decoration. Here, for the first time, can be found such characteristic Vijayanagara features as piers with cut-out colonettes and outsized rearing *yalis*. These fantastic animals are vigorously posed, with their front paws held up, and their fierce leonine heads have protruding eyes and fangs. *Makaras* (aquatic beasts) with crocodile-like snouts are seen beneath. The piers are overhung by a deep double-curved eave and surmounted by an exuberant brick and plaster parapet that forms part of the 19th-century renovation.

The interior of the *mandapa* presents a spacious open hall lined with sixteen animal piers; here, however, armed warriors ride the *yalis*. The ceiling above is carried on inverted T-shaped beams that span a distance of more than 8 metres. It is entirely covered with splendid paintings divided into panels, some of which portray the marriages of Virupaksha and Pampa, and Rama and Sita. Another pair of matching panels near the middle of the ceiling shows Shiva as riding in a chariot shooting an arrow at the demon rulers of the triple cities, represented here by three small circular forts, and Kama aiming one of his arrows at Shiva seated in

Painted ceiling in the coronation mandapa in the Virupaksha temple complex

meditation. The narrow panel at the extreme eastern end of the ceiling is of particular interest since it portrays Vidyaranya seated in a palanquin being carried in procession by attendants and soldiers. The accessory figures are dressed in costumes and bear guns and standards that cannot be much older than 200 years. Clearly the ceiling paintings belong to the early 19th-century phase of renovation, though it is possible that they replaced an original Vijayanagara period composition.

Today, devotees no longer enter the temple through the *mandapa* just described; instead they pass through the south porch to the inner *mandapa*, pausing at the doorway to the main sanctuary to pay reverence to Virupaksha. The god is represented as a *mukha-linga*, with an embossed brass facemask. Exiting by the north porch, devotees then proceed to visit the smaller shrines of Pampadevi and Bhuvaneshvari, situated immediately north of the Virupaksha sanctuary. The Bhuvaneshvari shrine appears to be of considerable antiquity, since it is built of grey-green chloritic schist columns, beams, ceiling slabs and perforated screens. However, these 10th- or 11th-century elements are no longer in their original context, having been removed from some dismantled temple and reassembled, presumably during the Vijayanagara era. Among the plethora of other minor shrines to be found around the main sanctuary is one dedicated to Mahishasuramardini (Durga slaying the buffalo demon) and another to Adishesha (primeval serpent associated with Vishnu), the latter being simply a shallow wall recess surrounded by an ornate plaster frame.

In order to proceed to the Tungabhadra from the temple, devotees usually exit by a large gate on the north side of the inner enclosure. Known locally as the Kanakagiri *gopura*, after the town 25 kilometres north of Hampi, its whitewashed tower was renovated in the 1830s by FW Robinson, then the District Collector of Bellary. Its granite lower portions, however, are an authentic Vijayanagara-period construction of the 15th century. Two inscribed slabs set up within its passageway are assigned to the 12th and 14th centuries.

Early style shrines overlooking Manmatha tank at Hampi

Manmatha tank

The Kanakagiri *gopura* leads directly to the Manmatha tank, once the principal bathing place for visitors to the Virupaksha complex, but now somewhat dilapidated, with many of the surrounding steps partly subsided. A cluster of small shrines overlooks its western bank, lining a path that proceeds northwards to the river. Among these is the Durgadevi shrine, the earliest intact structure at the site, being the only one built of sandstone.

Its simple pilastered walls and pyramidal tower capped by a *kuta* (square-to-domed) roof are typical of the Rashtrakuta style that was current in this part of Karnataka in the 9th century. (It is possible that the original Virupaksha shrine was of a similar appearance and date, but since this is now concealed within much later accretions it cannot be observed.) The front porch of the Durgadevi shrine, constructed of granite columns sheltered by sloping roof slabs, is an addition that may be contemporary with the inscribed slab set up here, bearing the date

1199. This record is the earliest to mention the worship of Pampa and Virupaksha at Hampi. The three-dimensional sculpted warrior battling a lion placed nearby is also a relic of the pre-Vijayanagara period, being assigned to the 13th-century Hoysala period. However, the multi-armed image of Durga, now worshipped in the sanctuary, is modern. Though other shrines of the group belong to the 13th and early 14th centuries, these are of lesser interest and are little used.

HEMAKUTA HILL & GANESHA MONOLITHS

The tour of Hampi continues by exiting the Virupaksha temple complex through the main entrance *gopura* and turning immediately right (south), following a stepped path that ascends Hemakuta hill. A simple 15th-century *gopura* entrance without a tower is soon seen on the right (west). This gives access to a group of small shrines within a fortified zone, with walls running

Shrines on Hemakuta hill dating from the pre- and early-Vijayanagara period

around the perimeter of the hill. These modest structures are the best-preserved examples of pre- and early-Vijayanagara period architecture at Vijayanagara. They are disposed somewhat dramatically on a sloping shelf of granite that rises steeply from the Virupaksha complex. Indeed, they were originally linked to the core Virupaksha shrine by a path that led from the Tungabhadra, past Manmatha tank and the Virupaksha shrine, and ascended through a series of pavilion-like gateways to the summit of the hill. When Krishnadevaraya expanded the Virupaksha shine into a vast complex in the

early 16th century, this pathway was cut off, yet the gateways still stand, including the double-storeyed example near the summit of the hill, from where there is a splendid panorama of the Tungabhadra valley.

The Hemakuta shrines display the typical Deccan architecture of the 13th and 14th centuries, with one or more shrines opening off a small square *mandapa*, entered through an open porch provided with angled seating slabs. Three of the larger temples each have triple shrines with unadorned walls topped with finely

Double-storeyed gateway at the top of Hemakuta hill (*top*)
Interior of shrine on Hemakuta hill (*above*)

worked granite towers that present pyramids of eave-like mouldings crowned with *kalasha* finials. One of the two north-facing examples of this type of temple is of historical significance because of the inscription on a pillar inside the *mandapa*. This records that the monument was built by Kampila, the early 14th-century king of the Hampi region, as a memorial for his parents and another relative. As in all the temples on the hill, the sanctuaries of Kampila's monument accommodate simple Shiva *lingas*. A nearby east-facing triple-shrined temple has contrasting pilastered walls and storeyed towers capped by *kuta* roofs in the typical Rashtrakuta manner, but it too is assigned to the early 14th century. Whether this and the other multiple *linga* shrine temples on the hill also served as royal memorials remains unknown, but it is tempting to interpret the Hemakuta

Columned mandapa of the Kadalekalu Ganesha shrine above Hampi

group as a commemorative Shaiva complex in which the first kings of Vijayanagara attempted to link themselves with their immediate predecessors in the region, such as Kampila (*see page 18*).

By steadily following the path up Hemakuta hill, visitors will eventually exit the fortified complex through a gateway, from which there is a framed view of Matanga hill. Beneath the gateway, near the junction of the roads running from Hampi to Hospet and Kamalapura, is a monolithic sculpture of a seated Ganesha sheltered by a columned *mandapa*. This 2.4-metre high image is known locally as Sasivekalu (mustard-seed) Ganesha.

A short distance away, at the top of the ridge overlooking Hampi, is a massive pavilion-like gateway with four passageways that controlled access to the original paved ramp leading down to Hampi, portions of which can still be seen. A few metres to the north stands an austere but elegant temple. Fronting it is an open *mandapa*, with 24 unusually slender

Sasivekalu Ganesha

columns, that offers a fine view of Hampi. The temple's sanctuary
accommodates a natural boulder sculpted with a huge, 4.5-metre high image
of a seated Ganesha. The trunk of the god reaches down to nuzzle a rice-cake
held in the right hand, while the massive belly protrudes outwards. This
monolith is popularly known today as Kadalekalu (gram) Ganesha.

Kadalekalu Ganesha in shrine above Hampi

KRISHNA TEMPLE COMPLEX & NARASIMHA MONOLITH

The tour described here continues southward along the road leading to Kamalapura. About 500 metres south of Hampi stands the Krishna temple complex, the nucleus of Krishnapura, another quarter of the sacred centre. It too is provided with a broad bazaar street extending to the east, but this is set at a lower level than the temple, where fields of sugarcane and bananas engulf its colonnades. A rectangular tank, surrounded by additional colonnades and with a small pavilion standing in the middle of the water, is picturesquely situated beneath a rocky overhang a few metres to the north of the street.

The grand scale of the entrance *gopura* proclaims the royal nature of the temple, which was erected in 1515 by Krishnadevaraya to commemorate his victory over the Gajapati rulers of Orissa and to accommodate a granite icon of the infant Krishna, looted on this occasion from the fort at Udayagiri in present-day Andhra Pradesh. (This image was removed from the temple and can now be seen in the Government State Museum, Chennai.) The *gopura* is now much dilapidated, but its frontal portico is impressive for the height of its columns (recently reset). The incompletely preserved brick tower rising above has remnants of plaster sculptures, including battle scenes that may depict the Orissa campaign (west face). Recent renovations have reworked and simplified the original figures. Doorway jambs within the *gopura* passageway are carved with

Entrance gopura of the Krishna temple complex, south of Hampi.

beautiful maidens clutching creepers, while a curious hare-in-the-moon motif between *nagas* can be seen on the under-side of one of the lintels above.

An inscribed slab set up in front of the main temple in the middle of the walled compound gives details of the Krishnadevaraya's military exploits and benefactions. Though somewhat hastily finished, judging from the poor quality of the carving, the monument is a typical example of 16th-century architecture. It consists of a 25-bay open *mandapa*, an enclosed nine-bay *mandapa* with side porches, and a towered sanctuary surrounded by an unlit passageway. Minor shrines are positioned near the outer corners, with a double-sanctuaried goddess temple to the north. The colonnade that runs

Interior of granary in the Krishna temple complex (*above left*). Monolithic *linga* next to the complex (*above right*)

around the perimeter wall is interrupted on the south side for a passageway that leads to an earlier pavilion-like gateway, later incorporated into the complex and provided with a brick tower. A break in the perimeter wall here gives access to the outer walled enclosure of the complex, in which stands a six-domed structure built of plaster-covered rubble, with arches on the inside. The building has steps to the roof where there are holes in the domes, indicating that it must have served as a granary.

The main road continues by winding through the outer enclosure of the Krishna complex and another early pavilion-like gateway with three passageways. Soon the road passes by a footpath leading to the monolithic Narasimha. This colossal statue, some 6.7 metres high, portrays the man-lion form of Vishnu seated in yogic posture beneath a multi-headed *naga* topped by a monster mask. The god has a horrific face, with protruding eyes and fangs, but is portrayed in an impassive mood together with his consort, Lakshmi. While almost nothing is left of the figure of this goddess, the head, legs and band secured around the knees of the god have all been renewed. Walls with doorway jambs, vestiges of a gigantic square chamber that was never finished, surround the monolith. An inscribed slab set up in front of the doorway records Krishnadevaraya's commission of 1528.

Next to the Narasimha is a monolithic *linga*, about 3 metres tall, standing on a circular pedestal. It is housed in a cubical chamber roofed with flat slabs.

UDDANA VIRABHADRA TEMPLE & CHHATRA

The road running towards Kamalapura continues southward, traversing
the lush fields of the irrigated valley, until it comes to a sharp bend, winding
around the Uddana Virabhadra temple. Just before the bend is an abandoned
16th-century Vaishnava temple with a finely finished portico with *yali* piers
facing directly onto the road. This gives access to a dilapidated and empty
sanctuary, near which is a low rock set within a crudely built chamber and
carved with a two-armed goddess, worshipped as Chamundeshvari (Kali), who
holds a ball of rice and a ladle.

    The Uddana Virabhadra temple on the other side of the road is a popular
venue for local weddings and is visited regularly by crowds of pilgrims Though
architecturally crude, the shrine houses an impressive, 3.6-metre high image of
Shiva as a fierce warrior, holding bow, arrow, sword and shield. Actually the
shrine was originally an open gateway through which the main road passed;
only in post-Vijayanagara times was it filled in to create the present temple.

    An interesting *sati* stone showing a deceased man in the company of his
three wives can be seen near the entrance gate in front. Possibly, he is the
military general who erected both the Vaishnava temple and the Virabhadra
image in 1545, as mentioned in the adjacent inscribed slab.

    Hidden away in the fields immediately to the west of the road that
winds around the Uddana Virabhadra temple is a vast colonnaded structure
with two raised galleries that functioned as a feeding-house, or *chhatra*.

Colonnades of the dilapidated *chhatra*

OCTAGONAL FOUNTAIN & BHOJANA SHALA

Continuing southward in the direction of Kamalapura, the road passes through a dismantled gateway in the urban core and begins to climb up to a ridge with remarkable granite formations, one of which is called the 'sister stones'. By continuing along this road and not turning left (east) on to an unpaved road leading to the royal centre, visitors will pass on the left (north)

a small octagonal domed fountain with arcades on all sides. Broken terracotta pipes in the vicinity once fed water to a fountain inside and to abandoned features to the south. A little further on the right (south) is the *bhojana shala*. This consists of green chloritic schist slabs carved with circular thali-like dishes on either side of a water channel, as if for an outdoor picnic spot for courtiers.

The road continues to the queens' bath and then on to the village of Kamalapura, but the itinerary described here follows the previously mentioned unpaved road running toward the royal centre.

Octagonal fountain on the road from Hampi to Kamalapura (*top*)
Bhojana shala (*left*)

'UNDERGROUND' TEMPLE & NOBLEMEN'S QUARTER

The tour of the royal centre begins with the 'underground' temple, so called because it was once partly buried, but it is now fully exposed by excavation. Set well below ground level, the temple's somewhat austere interior is usually partly flooded with water from the surrounding fields, compelling visitors to wade through its gloomy halls. It presents something of an architectural

Entrance *gopura* to the 'underground' temple dedicated to Virupaksha

labyrinth since it comprises a number of additions to a core sanctuary with a pyramidal stone tower that resembles the 14th-century shrines on Hemakuta hill. This core sanctuary is now empty, but an inscribed slab set up in an outer mandapa indicates that the temple was originally consecrated to Virupaksha. Considering its proximity to many of the residential structures of the royal centre, the 'underground' temple may have been used by members of the king's household. The complex is entered on the east through a rudimentary 15th-century *gopura* that, like the entrance *gopura* on Hemakuta hill, is devoid of any brick tower.

A short distance away, on the other side of the road, can be seen an excavated palace structure, of which only the masonry basement, plaster floor and lower portions of rubble walls survive. Footing blocks once supported wooden columns, but these have long since disappeared, together with the decorative plasterwork and wooden beams and ceiling. The palace is laid out

Recently excavated palace in noblemen's quarter

in a sequence of rising levels, the intermediate levels being arranged in a characteristic U-shape formation. It stands in the middle of a court bounded by service structures.

Exactly this scheme is found repeated in the group of palaces excavated to the north. From a position atop a nearby boulder can be seen some fifteen palace structures, clustered closely together without any overall planning, but with narrow lanes in between, thereby giving a good idea of a crowded elite residential quarter. Though labelled 'noblemen's quarter' by the archaeologists, no historical information has been found to identify those who once lived here. Even so, the evidence of water channels and a gymnasium, as well as Chinese porcelain and occasional items of gold jewellery, does indeed suggest that the inhabitants belonged to the Vijayanagara court. Little remains of the sumptuous architectural decoration other than the stone basements with friezes of dancing figures and the staircase balustrades with sculpted *yalis*.

Returning to the road, visitors will see to its south a domed pavilion elevated on a corner of one of the walled compounds. This structure has arched openings with balconies carried on lotus brackets, indicating that it may have served as a watchtower or pleasure pavilion. Clearing work beneath the boulders to the left (north) of the road, a short distance further on, has exposed the bases of circular and rectangular granaries.

From here the road soon comes to a T-junction. Taking the left-hand (northern) fork, visitors will soon come to a booth selling tickets to the *zenana* enclosure.

ZENANA ENCLOSURE

Though this high-walled compound is now generally known as the *zenana* enclosure, the label is misleading since it suggests that here lived the women of the Vijayanagara court. Given that the elephant stables and parade ground are nearby, this hardly seems possible; more likely, it was used by the Vijayanagara king or his commanders.

Roughly quadrangular in shape, the *zenana* enclosure is defined by slender tapering walls composed of granite blocks with irregular, but remarkably fine, jointing. The interior of the enclosure, which extends some 200 metres from west to east, is dotted with structures of different designs. To the left (north) is a vaulted rectangular hall, now used as an archaeological store. Its plain walls are broken only by small ventilation holes, suggesting that it may have been

Partly broken walls of the zenana enclosure

intended as an armoury or treasury, or perhaps as a gymnasium where courtiers could work up a sweat. An intricately perforated parapet surmounts the double-curved eave carried on masonry rafters with *naga* hoods at the ends. The interior has a floor at ground level surrounded by an elevated arcade.

Next are two excavated palace structures. The example to the left (north) is raised on a triple series of basement mouldings that are the most ornate of the series. That to the right (south) is set within a rectangular

pool, with boating scenes carved in relief on to the palace basement. The
Lotus Mahal, which dominates the enclosure, is one of the best-preserved
structures in the royal centre. In spite of its fanciful name, this building
probably served as a council chamber, as is indicated on the map of 1799.
The pavilion is laid out on a square *mandala*-like plan with symmetrical
projections on each side. The moulded stone basement on which the
pavilion is elevated, the double-curved eave sheltering the arches and the
cluster of nine pyramidal towers that rises above are all derived from
temple architecture. In contrast, the lobed arches surrounded by plaster
decoration and the interior domes and vaults are clearly sultanate in style.
These mixed origins make for a delightful blend of features that illustrates
the inventiveness of the Vijayanagara courtly style at its best. The upper

chamber was also intended for use as is indicated by an awkwardly
articulated staircase tower abutting one corner of the pavilion.

Watchtowers, built in a similar hybrid manner, are seen in the southeast
corner of the *zenana* enclosure and in the middle of the north wall. These also
employ temple-like eaves and towers in combination with sultanate-style
pointed arches and interior domes. A third tower at the northeast corner of
the enclosure is now partly ruined. Other features within the enclosure
include a deep tank for water storage, the remains of a rectangular granary and
the foundations of walls that may have created smaller internal compounds.

Upper chamber of the Lotus Mahal (*below*). Lotus Mahal (*facing page*). Octagonal watchtower in the zenana
enclosure and tower of the Madhava temple (*following pages*)

ELEPHANT STABLES & NEARBY STRUCTURES

A modest opening in the east wall of the *zenana* enclosure leads to a spacious plaza, probably used as a parade ground for troops and animals. This is overlooked from the east by the elephant stables, the most imposing courtly structure of the royal centre. The stables comprise a long line of eleven

Elephant stables on east side of the parade ground outside the zenana enclosure

chambers, each of which could accommodate two elephants. Alternating domes and twelve-sided vaults rising above the arched doorways are arranged symmetrically to either side of a central raised chamber that may have been intended for drummers and other musicians. Unfortunately, the pyramidal tower with its curving eaves above this musicians' chamber is now lost.

The structure overlooking the parade ground from the north is almost as impressive as the stables. It has an elevated gallery with eleven pointed arches with lobed profiles that could have served as a grandstand from which to enjoy the activities of the parade ground below. The interior of the building has a long narrow court at ground level surrounded by arcades, exactly as in the vaulted structure within the zenana enclosure, but here open to the sky. It is possible that this court was used for martial sports involving wrestlers, soldiers and animals. Certainly it could not have served as quarters for guards as has been suggested.

The west side of the parade ground contains a collapsed two-storey gateway, with raised platforms on either side; massive elephant balustrades lie nearby. Masses of rubble on the north and south sides of the parade ground indicate other service structures.

A short distance further to the south is the small walled Madhava temple complex, with two shrines, one recently restored but towerless, the other with a small brick tower rising above plain granite walls. Within the *mandapa* in front of the latter shrine is a 2.7-metre high Anjaneya slab, the largest at the

Structure with arcaded veranda on north side of the parade ground

site. How this heavy slab came to be placed here remains a mystery. Not far distant is the sunken Ellamma shrine where Kali is still worshipped. Both the temple complex and the Ellamma shrine face onto the road that leads in a northeasterly direction out of the royal centre.

A path to the rear (east) of the elephant stables leads to a group of structures standing in the middle of the newly developed fields about 150 metres away, which also face onto the road. One temple here is dedicated to the Jain *tirthankara* Parshvanatha and is dated 1426. A short distance further, a monumental gateway with a barbican enclosure marks the point at which the road passes through the outer walls of the royal centre. A boulder some distance to the north has an inscription referring to this gateway dating from the reign of Bukka. Of interest are the Muslim guardian figures with pointed beards and long tunics carved onto the doorway jambs. One of these jambs is now at the Archaeological Museum in Kamalapura (*see page 93*). From here, the road once continued until it exited the urban core by passing through Talarighat gate.

HAZARA RAMA TEMPLE

By returning to the unpaved road and continuing a few metres south from the zenana enclosure, visitors will arrive at the Hazara Rama, or 'thousand Ramas', temple at the core of the royal centre. Originally consecrated to Rama under the name Ramachandra, it served as a royal chapel for the Vijayanagara kings. Erected by Devaraya I in the early part of the 15th century, it is of outstanding interest for both the quality and subjects of its carvings. First to be noticed are the long lines of reliefs that wrap around the outer face of the compound walls of the temple complex. These depict processions of elephants, horses with Muslim attendants, and different military contingents

of soldiers. There are also women playing drums, dancing with sticks, and enjoying the water sports of the Vasantotsava festival. The animals, soldiers and women are all

Main shrine (left) and Ramayana reliefs (below) of the Hazara Rama temple

shown progressing towards seated kings, exactly as in contemporary accounts of the Mahanavami festival. The variety and realism of the carvings are such that no two figures or animals are shown exactly alike.

Rama giving his ring to Hanuman

The temple compound is entered on the east through a pavilion-like gateway devoid of any tower, but with fine images of Bhairava (fierce form of Shiva) and Mahishasuramardini carved on to the columns in the passageway. Immediately to the right (north) can be seen other reliefs on the inside face of the compound walls. These depict Ramayana episodes that read from left to right and from bottom to top.

The main temple, which stands in the middle of the compound, is approached through an open mandapa added in the 16th century. Its brick parapet has finely modelled plaster sculptures of gods and royal devotees. Beyond lies the portico of the original closed mandapa with rather squat columns topped by prominent double capitals in the typical 15th-century manner. A Sanskrit inscription beside the main doorway proclaims that Devaraya was protected by the goddess Pampa.

That Rama is the principal deity of the temple is obvious from the triple tiers of carvings on the *mandapa* walls, illustrating 108 scenes from the *Ramayana*. These proceed in a clockwise direction around the walls of the square *mandapa*. They begin with Valmiki telling the story to a seated king, and the fire sacrifice of Dasharatha (father of Rama), both at the northwest corner of the *mandapa*, and end with the triumphal coronation of Rama at Ayodhya, at the southwest corner. Several crucial scenes of the story are positioned beside doorways and at the corners: for example, Ravana transforms himself from a humble mendicant standing in front of Sita's hut into a multi-armed demon riding in an aerial chariot (southeast corner), and Hanuman leaps over the ocean to Lanka (north doorway).

A pair of additional *Ramayana* scenes on the antechamber walls of the temple is among the finest of the series: Rama giving his ring to Hanuman (south) and Sita giving her hair-jewel to Hanuman (north). The outer walls of the sanctuary itself are of interest for the finely articulated pilasters with lotus brackets that define the projections and fill the intervening recesses. The brick tower above, however, is poorly preserved.

In contrast with this sculptural profusion, the *mandapa* interior of the temple is somewhat austere. There are, however, four imposing columns with polished shafts covered with ornately carved compositions of the 24 aspects of Vishnu accompanied by several *Ramayana* characters. (The shafts are made of dolerite, a finely grained igneous rock not found at the site, perhaps from western Karnataka.) The sanctuary is empty, except for a pedestal with three holes, presumably to secure sculpted figures of Rama, Lakshmana and Sita that have long ago disappeared.

In the Hazara Rama compound is another, similar but smaller, temple with two sanctuaries that may have been dedicated to Narasimha and Lakshmi. Here, too, are several *Ramayana* scenes, but there are also episodes from the story of Narasimha and the demon Hiranyakashipu he is believed to have disembowelled. The storeyed brick towers of this smaller temple, with kuta and shala (rectangular vaulted) roofs, are better preserved than that of the main temple; sculptures of Narasimha and Lakshmi can be made out. The partly enclosed *mandapa* in front was added in the 16th century, as was the hall in the northeast corner of the compound, obscuring several of the *Ramayana* reliefs.

Significant axial alignments with the surrounding landscape confirm the pivotal role of the Hazara Rama temple and its *Ramayana* imagery in the mythical landscape of the city. Standing in the middle of the *mandapa* of the main temple, visitors can gaze out through the north porch and enclosure gateway to the summit of Matanga hill; similarly, Malyavanta hill is seen through the east doorway. As has already been mentioned, both hills are closely linked with the *Ramayana*. Another axial relationship seems to have existed between the Hazara Rama temple and its surrounding enclosures: a small doorway in the south perimeter wall leads to a walled alley that separates the enclosures linked with the public ceremonial activities of the king (east) from those intended as more private and residential zones (west).

A short distance east of the Hazara Rama temple compound is a reconstructed *dipa-stambha* and a small Hanuman shrine. An adjacent pond has inclined seating slabs all around. Other dilapidated structures here flank the beginning of the road that leads through an arched gateway in a northeasterly direction out of the royal centre.

West of the hazara rama temple

Further features of interest are seen in the enclosures west of the Hazara Rama temple where the archaeologists have exposed palace structures of the type already noted in the noblemen's quarter. (One of these enclosures has imaginatively but inaccurately been labelled 'the mint'.) Several of the palaces and their associated subsidiary structures are only reached by following complicated routes of access, with many turns of direction through intermediate gateways and courts. Much better preserved are two adjacent, sultanate-style structures: one a two-storeyed octagonal pavilion, the other, a nine-domed reception hall facing north.

Excavated palace structure west of the Hazara Rama temple (*top*). Two-storeyed octagonal pavilion (*centre*). Interior of nine-domed hall (*right*)

AUDIENCE HALL, MAHANAVAMI
PLATFORM & TANKS

Passing through the two gateway structures south
of the Hazara Rama temple, a walled enclosure is
reached that measures roughly 300 by 250 metres.
This quadrangular enclosure - once subdivided into
smaller areas - is by far the largest in the royal
centre and the only one to contain identifiable
ceremonial structures. First to be seen is the
audience hall with 100 stone footing blocks.
Presumably these supported massive wooden
columns that were burnt when the city was sacked
and of which no trace can now be seen, though it
is tempting to speculate on their original
sumptuous appearance. The floor of this hall is
raised on a high but unadorned double basement
with a later elevated platform to the west and a
staircase on the south ascending to a vanished
upper level. To the south of the hall is a cluster of
smaller and lower square and rectangular platforms,
separated one from another by small courts, one of which is paved with
chloritic schist or white limestone slabs. To the southeast is an underground

chamber lined with chloritic schist columns and wall slabs taken from a dismantled 11th- or 12th-century temple; this may have functioned as a subterranean treasury. A short distance to the east of the chamber is a reconstructed basement with fine carvings. Several wells and pools are also seen in this area.

Dominating the entire enclosure is a square, multi-stage platform that occupies the northeast corner, one of the highest points in this zone, and from which there is a fine panoramic view of the royal centre. The lower two granite stages of the platform probably date from the foundation of the royal centre in the 14th century. They are covered with shallow reliefs illustrating a full range of royal activities carved in a rudimentary but vigorous style that is unique in the art of Vijayanagara. Here kings are depicted giving audience, watching wrestling matches, hunting deer and stabbing leopards. Foreigners with pointed hats, most likely Central Asian Turks, lead horses, hold clubs and play tambourines. Lines of elephants, horses and camels, and even the

Mahanavami platform surrounded by walls and rubble (*above*). Steps ascending to the vanished upper level of the audience hall (*facing page*)

occasional mythical animal, make an appearance. A staircase on the south, flanked by relief carvings that include rows of female stick-dancers, leads to the eastern side of the platform, where a double staircase climbs to the top of the third stage, also in granite but with few carvings. The column footings that can be seen on top indicate a grand wooden *mandapa*, with broad central aisles oriented to the cardinal directions. The west face of the platform was remodelled in the 16th century with the addition of tiers of chloritic schist mouldings. Badly damaged and wrongly reassembled, the surviving mouldings preserve only traces of their original carvings, though several royal couples, a battle procession and scenes of the Vasantotsava festival with courtly women throwing water at each other can still be made out. None of the topics illustrated on the monument are specifically linked with the Mahanavami, but the platform is popularly believed to have been the place where the king made sacrifices to a divinity in the course of this festival.

Several metres south of the platform is a raised channel that conducted water into the enclosure. It also fed a square stepped tank, which was discovered only in the 1980s. The pool at its bottom can be reached by descending symmetrically disposed flights of steps with landings that create complex patterns enhanced by light and shade. The blocks are inscribed with numbers and letters indicating directions, suggesting the possibility that the tank was dismantled at some far-off site and transported piece by piece to the capital where it was reassembled. A short distance away is a much larger rectangular tank, more than 60 metres long, probably intended for courtly water entertainments. Other smaller pools in the area were perhaps used for royal ceremonies.

Side walls and staircase balustrade of the Mahanavami platform *(top)*, with a detail of one of the blocks showing a royal hunter and deer in relief *(above)*

QUEENS' BATH, CHANDRASHEKHARA TEMPLE & OCTAGONAL BATH

This tour of the royal centre concludes with a description of the queens' bath outside the walled enclosures in the extreme southeast corner of this zone, next to the main road leading from Hampi to Kamalapura. Though known as the queens' bath, this water pavilion was probably intended for male courtiers and their female companions. The structure presents a severely plain exterior, which contrasts markedly with the interior where

there is a delightful arcaded corridor roofed with ornate vaults of different designs running around a square pool, now sadly lacking any water. Balconies with arched windows, once decorated with delicate plasterwork, project over the pool. Towers that at one time rose above the roof, as recorded in an early watercolour (*see page 7*), have now been lost. A water channel surrounds the structure, and some distance away to the east and north are the remains of a collapsed aqueduct that formed part of the extensive water supply system of the royal centre.

A short distance to the east of the queens' bath is the 16th-century

Queens' bath showing balconies projecting over central pool, now devoid of water

Chandrashekhara (Shiva) temple. This stands in an enclosure contained within newly repaired walls interrupted by a small *gopura* on the east. The temple has two shrines but there is no information about the deities who were installed here. About 100 metres to the north is a much smaller temple

perched picturesquely on a boulder. This once housed an image of Tiruvengalanatha.

Also to be found in this area is an octagonal colonnade surrounding a similarly shaped pool with an island platform. Recent excavations nearby have exposed the walls and basements of two large palace complexes. An even more elaborate complex has been cleared a short distance to the north, next to a rock-cut shrine.

Small Tiruvengalanatha temple (left).
Octagonal bath (below)

ARCHAEOLOGICAL MUSEUM & PATTABHIRAMA TEMPLE COMPLEX

Shortly after the queens' bath, the main road passes through a crudely reconstructed gateway in the outer walls of the urban core, from where it continues until it reaches a junction on the outskirts of Kamalapura. This village is mainly of interest for the Archaeological Museum, which has an open court with an instructive large-scale model of the site. Among the sculptures on display in the galleries around the court are reliefs of Virabhadra, Anjaneya and Garuda, several slender *nagakals* (snake stones) and portraits of a courtly couple in royal costume, now headless (*see page 21*). Coins and inscriptions can also be seen. The well-landscaped garden stores a host of *sati* stones. (The museum is open daily, except Fridays, from 10.00 am to 5.00 pm; the entrance fee is Rs 5.)

The Pattabhirama temple, beside the road leading east from Kamalapura, is about 600 metres from the museum. Dedicated to Rama, it once formed the nucleus of a suburban quarter known as Varadadevi-ammana-pattana after one of the queens of Achyutaraya. (This quarter was totally destroyed when a power plant was constructed in the

Doorway jamb showing Muslim guard, from the gateway to the east of the elephant stables; Archaeological Museum, Kamalapura

Open mandapa in front of the Pattabhirama temple

1950s.) Indeed, this emperor may have built the complex, which is one of the largest at the site, but no records are preserved of its founding patron. The temple itself, which consists of the standard sequence of open *mandapa*, enclosed *mandapa* with side porches, and sanctuary surrounded by a passageway, stands in the middle of a vast paved courtyard. Lacking fine sculptural detail, the temple is nevertheless impressive for its scale, elegant proportions and long elevation. A 100-columned hall, now damaged, is built up to the south wall of the spacious enclosure, while a *gopura* with a well-preserved brick tower is positioned on the east.

A short distance north of the Pattabhirama temple is a portion of the walls of the urban core of the city, into which is set a gateway with a lofty pointed dome carried on four arches. This once served as the major point of entry into the urban core from the southeast.

The tour continues by returning to Kamalapura and taking the road that runs north, passing through the walls to enter the urban core, and continuing to Talarighat.

Domed gateway leading into the urban core

GANAGITTI JAIN TEMPLE & BHIMA'S GATE

The first monument of interest to be noticed along this road is the Ganagitti Jain temple, one of the largest early edifices at the site. The temple, which has duplicated shrines and *mandapas*, is built in an austere style with plain outer walls and a stepped pyramidal stone tower over one of the sanctuaries. The interior is notable for the finely worked but somewhat squat columns with prominent double capitals. An inscription of 1385 on the lofty *dipa-stambha* in front records that the temple was built by Irugappa, a general of Harihara II. A short walk along a pathway to the rear (east) leads to Bhima's gate in the perimeter walls of the urban core. Slabs carried on tiers of lotus brackets roof the gate. It is shielded by a spacious barbican enclosure creating a bent entryway, inside which is a slab carved with the *Mahabharata* hero after whom the gate takes its name.

Ganagitti Jain temple (*below*) Relief carving of Bhima inside Bhima's gate (*right*)

MALYAVANTA HILL

The road soon comes to a fork, with the right-hand (eastern) road leading towards Kampli village. It is worth following this road for about 600 metres since it passes beneath Malyavanta hill, at the summit of which is the Raghunatha temple, of considerable interest for its *Ramayana* associations. This well-preserved complex has *gopuras* on the east and the south, the latter provided with a frontal portico employing finely carved yali piers. Its plan is similar to the larger but ruined eastern gateway of the Krishna temple complex. Fine plaster decoration and bands of colour are seen in the tower that rises above. Serpents, fish, tortoises and other fanciful aquatic creatures are carved in shallow relief on the enclosure walls. The sanctuary of the main temple abuts a rock carved with a scene showing Rama and Sita together with Lakshmana and Hanuman. The rock protrudes above the roof of the temple where it is topped by a small, partly reconstructed tower. The 100-columned hall on the south side of the enclosure is complete, with all of its internal piers and ceiling slabs intact. A small doorway in the rear (west) wall of the compound leads to a rocky shelf, from where there is a fine view over the urban core. A natural crevice here is lined with reliefs of small *lingas* and Nandis.

Cleft with relief carvings of lingas and Nandis on the hill

AHMAD KHAN'S MOSQUE & TOMB & TALARIGHAT GATE

Returning to the road that runs from Kamalapura to Talarighat and proceeding for about 750 metres before taking a faintly marked path to the left (west), visitors may visit the surviving monuments of one of the Islamic quarters of the urban core. Here stand a mosque, a tomb and an octagonal well built in 1439 by Ahmad Khan, a military officer in the service of Devaraya II. The mosque is like a rudimentary *mandapa* with squat columns, but has a prayer niche in the rear wall, while the adjacent tomb has arched niches and a dome. The plaster that once coated these buildings with a fine finish is now lost. Other tombs and graveyards are seen nearby, on either side of an abandoned roadway.

The modern road continues northward, crossing the Turuttu canal that runs along the irrigated valley, before passing through Talarighat gate and leaving the urban core. Part of an upper chamber of the gate survives, a portion of its walls with arched windows topped by a parapet of battlements.

From here it is less than a kilometre to Talarighat, the river crossing to Anegondi. The itinerary described from now on, however, takes the unpaved road to the left (west) leading to the Vitthala temple complex.

Talarighat gate (*right*)
Ruined façade of Ahmad Khan's mosque (*top*)

VITTHALA TEMPLE COMPLEX

The first structure to be noticed on this road is a small *mandapa* with a central dais, above which rises a brick tower. Though now standing picturesquely in the midst of fields, this structure originally marked the end of the great paved and colonnaded street that ran for almost a kilometre eastward from the Vitthala temple complex. The *mandapa* was used to display the processional image of the god carried in a chariot that was pulled up and down the street. Continuing along the road, the surviving colonnades of the chariot street start to appear, into which are set a temple on the left (south) and a portico further along on the right (north). Both these structures employ piers carved with rearing horses, the only examples of this animal motif at Vijayanagara. They date from the last phase of building activity towards the middle of the 16th century. The portico gives access to a large rectangular tank surrounded by steps, with a small pavilion in the middle. Ahead, at the end of the street, can be seen the principal *gopura* of the temple complex, the nucleus of Vitthalapura, one of the principal quarters of Vijayanagara's sacred centre.

Considered a masterpiece of temple architecture at Vijayanagara, the Vitthala is an historical enigma since nothing is known about the circumstances under which it was originally built. Some scholars date it to the

Tank with colonnades and central pavilion near the Vitthala temple complex

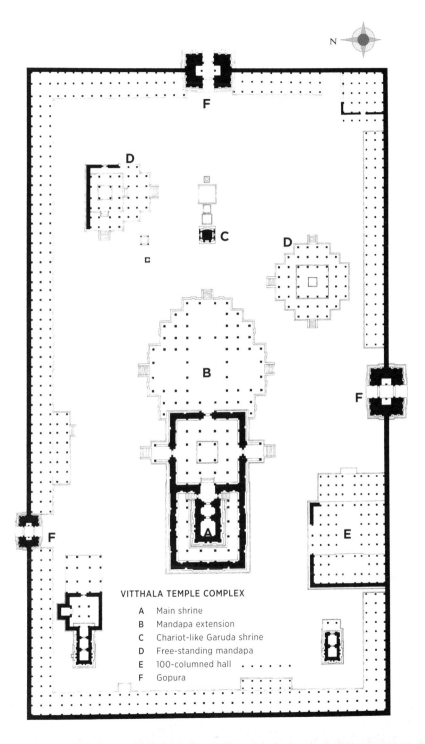

VITTHALA TEMPLE COMPLEX

A   Main shrine
B   Mandapa extension
C   Chariot-like Garuda shrine
D   Free-standing mandapa
E   100-columned hall
F   Gopura

late 15th century; more likely, it is a Tuluva-period foundation of the early 16th century, to which the later emperors of this dynasty, together with their queens, courtiers and officers, all made gifts and structural additions. The temple stands in a vast rectangular courtyard with *gopuras* on three sides. Two queens of Krishnadevaraya built the gopuras on the east and north in 1513, while that on the south is a later and more ornate structure. The main shrine was built in two phases, beginning with a spacious enclosed *mandapa*, recently restored, leading to a sanctuary with a small brick tower surrounded by a passageway. The sanctuary is now empty, its doorway and ceiling fractured by fire, evidence of the destruction wreaked on the monument. Its outer walls, however, as viewed with some difficulty from within the unlit passageway, preserve delicately modelled basement mouldings and wall pilasters.

The later phase of construction of the Vitthala temple is represented by the magnificent, though much damaged, open *mandapa* added in 1554 by one of Sadashiva's military commanders. The structure is laid out on a complex plan with numerous projections. It is raised on an ornate basement,

with relief carvings showing Europeans and other figures leading horses, interrupted by miniature niches accommodating the *avataras* of Vishnu, as well as by flights of steps flanked by animal balustrades. The glory of the *mandapa* is the treatment of the piers fashioned with remarkable skill out of single granite blocks. (The clustered cut-out colonettes that surround the shafts emit tones when tapped lightly; however, contrary to popular belief, the tones do not form part of a musical scale.) The piers are sheltered by a deep double-curved eave with rings for lamp chains at the corners and pseudo-rafters on the under-side; portions of an ornate brick parapet can be seen above. The interior of the *mandapa* is divided into four spacious halls, each surrounded by piers with additional colonettes, *yalis* and diverse figures, including musicians (east hall) and multiple aspects of Narasimha (north hall). Massive brackets and beams rise above, supporting lofty ceilings composed of solid granite slabs, some with spans exceeding 10 metres. These upper portions are almost completely preserved in the north and south halls, including the inverted T-shaped beams that carry the elaborately carved ceiling slabs.

Interior passageway around the sanctuary (*top*)
Outer walls and tower of the main shrine of the
Vitthala temple complex (*left*)

Garuda shrine in the form of a wheeled chariot in the Vitthala temple complex

Immediately in front (east) of the temple stands a chariot-like structure with pairs of wheels on the sides and a small Garuda shrine with exquisite cut-out colonettes above. Its original brick tower, which appears in an early photograph (*see page 151*), was removed at the end of the 19th century. The striding elephants beneath the shrine doorway were also placed here at this time. Horses were originally intended; their tails can still be made out. Two free-standing *mandapas* are seen near the Garuda shrine. That on the south is the finest, being a perfectly symmetrical pavilion, with outer piers on four sides carved with *yalis* ridden by warriors in courtly dress or Muslim costume. The interior has a raised dais surrounded by further yali piers that carry an elevated lotus ceiling. In the northern *mandapa* a finely worked dais abuts the north wall. Both *mandapas* as well as the chariot-shrine are probably contemporary with the 1554 addition to the main temple. However, the 100-columned hall, built up to the enclosure wall next to the south *gopura*, has a Krishnadevaraya inscription that is dated 1516. This is a trilingual record with Kannada, Telugu and Tamil characters incised onto the outer walls.

In addition to the colonnaded street that proceeds eastward from the temple, there is another shorter one that runs north towards a walled temple

King's balance with two-storeyed gateway beyond

complex entered through a towerless *gopura* with a frontal porch. *Ramayana* carvings are seen on the walls of the gateway, while inside the temple *mandapa*, piers carved with yalis carry an elevated ceiling. Though historical data are lacking, this monument was probably dedicated to Ramanuja. Other religious edifices surrounding the Vitthala complex were associated with other alvars, and include the Tirumangai Alvar temple of 1556 near its northwest corner, and another, almost identical, temple aligned with its south *gopura*. The profusion of decaying *mandapas*, colonnades, *mathas*, kitchens, wells and *chhatras* in the vicinity testify to an active urban quarter linked with the cult of the alvars and the life of the Vitthala temple. Further evidence of a residential population is provided by decaying rubble walled structures and mortars for processing food.

The tour described here now takes the footpath running parallel to the Tungabhadra, leaving Vitthalapura through a double-storeyed pavilion-like gateway. Just before the gateway is the kings' balance, where the Vijayanagara emperors are traditionally believed to have had themselves weighed against gold and precious stones that were then distributed to temple brahmins. The balance consists of two posts and a lintel with a stone ring to take a metal chain.

SUGRIVA'S CAVE & NARASIMHA TEMPLE

The footpath that proceeds from the Vitthala temple complex towards Hampi
partly follows the top of the old fortifications; it offers distant views of the
Tungabhadra, including the granite pylons of a Vijayanagara bridge set into
the swirling water of the river. Downstream from the bridge is a massive
mandapa that has come to be associated with Purandaradasa, the celebrated
musician of the 16th-century Vijayanagara court and founder of the Karnatak
school of music.

   Soon the footpath passes by some boulders with a crevice painted
with white and ochre stripes to the right (north). This is known as Sugriva's
cave, from its association with the *Ramayana* episode. A nearby pool is called
Sitasarovar. On a hill that rises to the left (south) is a temple approached by a
long flight of steps. Dedicated to Narasimha, this early-style monument has a
sanctuary topped by a pyramid of eave-like mouldings, as in the Hemakuta
hill shrines. The sanctuary is preceded by a *mandapa* with side entrances
flanked by relief carvings of Hanuman and Garuda; the columns inside have
finely finished circular capitals. From here there is a splendid panorama of the
entire Tungabhadra valley, including a distant prospect of the principal *gopura*
of the Virupaksha temple at Hampi.

Gateway to the Narasimha temple overlooking the Tungabhadra

Tiruvengalanatha (Achyutaraya's) temple complex

Continuing along the footpath, visitors soon come to the end of the
colonnaded street leading to the Tiruvengalanatha temple, the core of
Achyutapura, another quarter of the sacred centre of Vijayanagara. Standing at
the end of the street, near the river, is a walled temple complex entered
through a towerless *gopura* on the east. This gateway is of interest for the
Vijayanagara dynastic emblems, showing boar and sword, carved onto its
passageway walls.

The Tiruvengalanatha monument, now much ruined, was built in 1534,
not by Achyutaraya, as its popular name suggests, but by his brother-in-law,
Hiriya Tirumalaraja. As with the other great religious complexes of this part of
the city, the monument stands at the end of a bazaar street, but here this runs
north towards the river, between Gandhamadana hill to the east and Matanga
hill to the west. The street is now much dilapidated, though the original
paving stones have been partly exposed. Two piles of blocks next to the
colonnades on opposite sides of the street, not far from the temple entrance,
once served as chariot landings. Behind the western colonnade can be seen a
large but decaying rectangular tank surrounded by steps with a small pavilion
in the middle.

Ruined west *gopura* of the Tiruvengalanatha temple complex

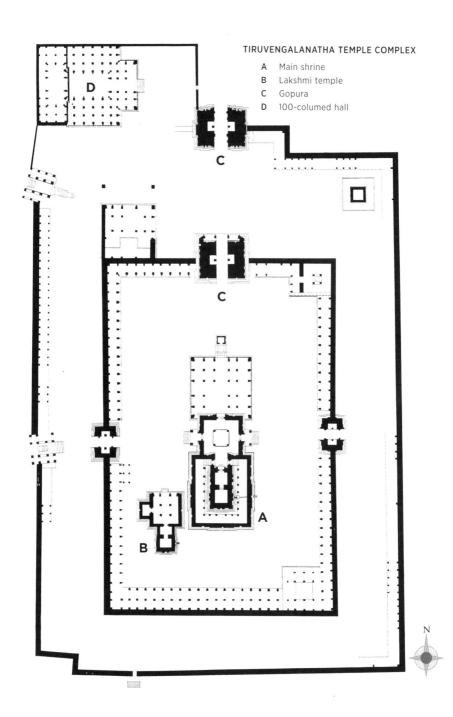

TIRUVENGALANATHA TEMPLE COMPLEX

A   Main shrine
B   Lakshmi temple
C   Gopura
D   100-columed hall

N

The temple complex is entered through a pair of almost identical *gopuras* of the standard type, with pilastered granite lower walls and pyramidal towers of brick and plaster, now incomplete. A portico on the front (north) face distinguishes the inner gateway. Fine carvings of Vaishnava deities and emblems adorn the jambs of the passageways of both *gopuras*. Inside the passageways are inscriptions specifying the donor and naming the deity to whom the complex was dedicated. These *gopuras* lead into a pair of concentric rectangular enclosures, at the core of which is the main temple, an arrangement that represents a significant advance in temple design. (This layout can best be appreciated from the roof of the Virabhadra shrine at the summit of Matanga hill.) The temple itself consists of a standard sequence of open *mandapa*, closed *mandapa* with side porches, and sanctuary surrounded by unlit passageway. A Lakshmi shrine with *yali* carvings on its porch columns stands to the southwest. Other worthwhile sculptures are found on the pillars in the 100-columned hall that occupies the northwest corner of the outer enclosure.

A small doorway in the rear (south) outer enclosure wall of the complex leads to a pathway that runs past an impressive rock carving of Kali, now under worship and brightly painted. The pathway continues beside a modern channel feeding irrigated fields to the base of a granite staircase that climbs to the top of Matanga hill.

Two pathways are found on the western side of the Tiruvengalanatha temple complex: one leads to a somewhat precarious stairway ascending to the summit of Matanga hill; the other proceeds over the ridge and through a gateway before descending into the Hampi bazaar.

Painted rock carving of Kali near the Tiruvengalanatha temple complex

KODANDARAMA TEMPLE & RIVERSIDE SCULPTURES

Only a short distance further along the footpath that follows the river is the
Kodandarama temple. This overlooks Chakratirtha, the holiest bathing spot
on the Tungabhadra, situated at a point where the river makes a turn
northward to flow through a rugged gorge. In front of the temple is a *dipa-
stambha* sheltered by a spreading *pipal* tree, the trunk of which is surrounded by
nagakals. Pilgrims visit the Kodandarama temple to worship the relief
composition of Rama with Sita accompanied by Lakshmana and Hanuman
carved onto a natural boulder set within the sanctuary. This is approached
through a double porch with *yali* columns. Several lesser shrines can be seen
at a higher elevation to the rear (south). One shrine, originally dedicated
to Vitthala, has an early-style sanctuary topped by a plain pyramidal roof. A
second shrine is built up to a boulder carved with a delicately modelled
composition, almost a metre across, showing Anjaneya inside an eight-pointed
star. A third shrine accommodates the flaming discus weapon of Vishnu.

A path running north from the Kodandarama temple leads to Kotitirtha
in the Tungabhadra gorge. By scrambling over the rocks, visitors will
come across several unusual boulder reliefs, including two large *mandalas*
composed of miniature *lingas*, and a fine depiction of Anantashayana
(reclining Vishnu). A set of carvings portraying the 24 forms of Vishnu as
well as episodes from the story of Narasimha and Hiranyakashipu are found

Priests at the Kodandarama temple

on a rock face above. A small sanctuary nearby, built on the very edge of the river, is of interest for the fine reliefs of donor figures and diverse deities, although these have recently been vandalized.

The pathway continues beside the colonnades and *ghats* above Chakratirtha, and then winds its way through and around boulders beside the Tungabhadra. Within only a few minutes, the Hampi bazaar street is reached.

Sculpture of Ranganatha in Tungabhadra gorge (*top*). Pavilion overlooking Tungabhadra gorge (*centre*) Mandala of miniature *lingas* carved on a boulder next to the Tungabhadra (*above*)

END OF HAMPI BAZAAR STREET & MATANGA HILL

Turning left (east) on arriving at the bazaar street, visitors quickly arrive at its terminus, some 750 metres distant from the entrance *gopura* of the Virupaksha complex that is visible at the other end. Several structures are grouped here, including a double-storeyed *mandapa* with reused 12th-century chloritic schist columns intended for ceremonies associated with the chariot festivals. It has now been converted into a stage by the addition of a concrete platform and an unsightly steel frame. A reconstructed *mandapa* nearby now serves as a museum to display early photographs of the site. Beneath the boulders to the north of the extreme end of the street is an open *mandapa* housing a colossal seated Nandi monolith, the head of which is damaged. A stepped path beside the Nandi leads up and over the ridge to the Tiruvengalanatha complex.

A short distance back towards Hampi, another path turns left (south) towards Matanga hill. This winds around the hill until it arrives at the foot of the southern flank, where begins a granite staircase dating from

Vijayanagara times and still in remarkably good condition. The summit of Matanga is marked by a sanctuary dedicated to Virabhadra surrounded by dilapidated *mandapas* and courtyards. The view from the top of the hill gives the best possible idea of the layout of the entire city, including the sacred centre, irrigated valley and royal centre. An early morning ascent is recommended.

Visitors have now to walk back along the bazaar street towards the Virupaksha complex. Along the way they will notice several *mandapas* with double-height columns topped with elaborate parapets. They can be associated with the early 19th-century renovation of Hampi and may have been intended for temporary use by important visitors during chariot festivals. Today they serve as residences for squatters, as do many of the colonnades on either side. As visitors proceed towards the temple, the bazaar street narrows because of the shops, stores and hotels, until the entrance *gopura* of the main complex is reached and the itinerary described here comes to an end.

Virabhadra shrine on top of Matanga hill (*above*)
Pavilions and gateway at the end of the Hampi bazaar street (*left*)

KADIRAMPURA, MALPANNAGUDI & ANANTASHAYANAGUDI

Apart from Kamalapura, the outlying suburban centres that survive as villages
in the Hampi region have not been covered by the circular tour just described.
The vestiges found here give some idea of the importance of these centres in
Vijayanagara times.

Kadirampura, which lies on the road leading from Hampi to Hospet,
is home to a recently renovated temple dedicated to Shiva's son,
Murugan, decorated with brightly painted plaster sculptures. The local patron
was also responsible for erecting the octagonal *samadhi* just outside the village,

Modern temple in Kadirampura

towards Hampi. This memorial, dedicated to his wife, consists of an octagonal
pavilion adorned with realistic human and animal figures. Of greater historical
interest are the two Muslim tombs that stand beside the road on the other side
of the village, towards Hospet. The larger example, now missing its dome, is
typical of 14th- or 15th-century Bahmani architecture, suggesting contacts
between Vijayanagara and the sultanate kingdom at this time. Nothing is
known about those who were buried here.

The road continues in the direction of Hospet, passing through
Malpannagudi, at either end of which are pavilion-like gateways marking the
ancient road. (One of these now serves as garage for the local chariot.) The
temple in the middle of Malpannagudi is a Vijayanagara-period foundation,
but was badly damaged when converted in later times into a small fort. Also of

interest is the step-well located beside the road, about 500 metres outside the village in the direction of Hospet. Dated 1412, this octagonal well is surrounded by sultanate-style arcades and is reached by a descending flight of steps.

Anantashayanagudi, the next village on the Hospet road, takes its name from the religious monument erected here in 1524 by Krishnadevaraya. The enclosure is entered from the north through a *gopura* of ambitious proportions that was never completed. The temple is unique in having a large rectangular sanctuary entered through triple doorways. This was intended to accommodate an image of Vishnu reclining on the cosmic serpent

Tower of Anantashayana temple (*above*)
Octagonal well near Malpannagudi (*top*)

Ananta, probably composed of plaster-covered brickwork, of which nothing can be seen now other than its long granite pedestal. However, the great vaulted roof with unusual semicircular ends rising some 24 metres above is still intact, though somewhat restored on the outside. The sanctuary is preceded by a spacious *mandapa* with lofty columns.

HOSPET

A royal suburb, founded by Krishnadevaraya and named Tirumaladevi-ammana-pattana after his principal queen, has entirely disappeared beneath the dusty streets of modern Hospet (including the palace where the emperor met with Domingo Paes). About the only historical feature to be seen in the vicinity is the great *bund* about a kilometre to the south of the town, and across which runs the traffic of National Highway 13. The stone-faced earthen dam was intended to trap water in a tapering valley between two ridges of the Sandur hills, but apparently never functioned successfully. (It is tempting to identify this tank with the one under construction observed by Paes; *see page 128.*)

ANEGONDI

By the far the best preserved of Vijayanagara's suburban centres is Anegondi, the history of which spans a longer period than that of the capital itself. Anegondi was an important fortified town in pre-Vijayanagara times and it is likely that the first Sangamas were based here before the foundation of their new capital. Anegondi continued to be a royal town in later times and still serves as the residence of a local line of rajas who claim descent from the Vijayanagara emperors.

Until the highway bridge currently under construction is completed, Anegondi is reached most conveniently from the Vijayanagara side of the Tungabhadra by circular coracles, the traditional means of river transport in this part of Karnataka. The journey passes by boulders in the middle of the water sculpted with Nandi and Ganesha images. The walls that encircle Anegondi are still evident, though on the east they form part of the *ghats* leading down to the Tungabhadra. The town preserves many traditional houses with wooden pillars, mud-clad walls and flat plastered roofs. In the middle is the palace complex of the Anegondi rajas, now much dilapidated though it is mostly no older than the 19th century.

Sculpted Nandi, *linga* and Ganesha on a rock in the middle of the Tungabhadra

Gagan Mahal overlooking the town square of Anegondi.

The main focus of the town is a square onto which faces the small
Ranganatha temple (dedicated to Anantashayana), of interest for several
reused and brightly painted 12th-century columns. On the opposite side of
the square is the Gagan Mahal, built in a typical late-Vijayanagara courtly
style with arched windows and pyramidal towers, now accommodating the
local council office. A 14th-century gateway marks the northern exit of the
town. Another interesting early structure is the Jain temple facing onto the
main street running south from the square. It was erected in 1402 by Irugappa,

the same general who
was responsible for the
Ganagitti temple in the
urban core of the
capital.

A complex of
shrines known as
Chintamani is built up
to the boulders to the
southeast of Anegondi
from where there is a
fine view of the
Tungabhadra. Yet other

Jain temple at Anegondi

structures stand within the fortified citadel that occupies the rocky hill a short distance west of the town. They include gateways, barracks, step-wells and royal memorials, all dating from the post-Vijayanagara period.

The road running west from Anegondi passes along the top of the ancient walls of the town, in which an early-style gateway with finely carved columns still stands. About 1.5 kilometres to the west, a cart track leads southward to Pampasarovar, the pool that takes its name from the Hampi goddess. A little further on is the access path to Anjenadri hill, which lies to the north of the road. Considered the birthplace of Anjaneya, this hill is a favourite place of pilgrimage and has a long staircase ascending to a modern shrine at the top.

Gateway to the fort above Anegondi

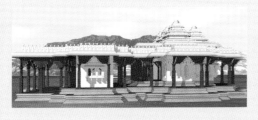

RECONSTRUCTIONS

These computer reconstructed images are an attempt to visualize the original appearance of Vijayanagara's ruined buildings by restoring damaged portions and adding elements that were burnt when the city was sacked or which decayed after the site was abandoned.

Audience hall: here the missing 100 wooden columns have been added, together with their ornamental brackets supporting a flat roof

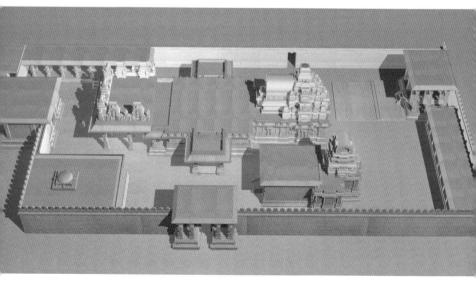

Hazara Rama temple: Aerial view of the complex from the north showing the walls enclosing the two shrines and auxiliary structures

Water palace in the *zenana* enclosure: The palace is shown complete with colonnaded veranda and pyramidal tower standing in the middle of a small pool

Large palace in the *zenana* enclosure: the vanished rooms with plastered rubble walls encased in a veranda with wooden cloumns are situated on the moulded stone basement

Queens' bath: the interior is filled with water overlooked by ornamental balconies and a tower rising above the parapet

Mahanavami platform: a hall with wooden columns and brackets is shown rising above the multi-stage masonry platform. Its flat roof is relieved by an ornamental parapet

APPENDIX

REPORTS OF FOREIGN VISITORS

ALEXANDER GREENLAW PHOTOGRAPHS

REPORTS OF FOREIGN VISITORS

NICOLO CONTI

Conti, an Italian traveller, is the author of the earliest known description (c. 1420) of
Vijayanagara by a foreign visitor. He was at the capital just after the accession of Devaraya I.

Departing hence, and travelling about three hundred miles inland [from Goa], we arrived at the great city of Bizenegalia [Vijayanagara], situated near very steep mountains. The circumference of the city is sixty miles; its walls are carried up to the mountains and enclose the valleys at their foot, so that its extent is thereby increased. In this city there are estimated to be ninety thousand men fit to bear arms. Their king is more powerful than all the other kings of India. He takes to himself twelve thousand wives, of whom four thousand follow him on foot wherever he may go, and are employed solely in the service of the kitchen. A like number, more handsomely equipped, ride on horseback.

In Bizenegalia also, at a certain time of the year, their idol is carried through the city, placed between two chariots, in which are young women richly adorned, who sing hymns to the god, and accompanied by a great concourse of people. Many, carried away by the fervour of their faith, cast themselves on the ground before the wheels, in order that they may be crushed to death. Others, making an incision in their side, and inserting a rope thus through their body, hang themselves to the chariot by ways or ornament, and thus suspended and half dead accompany their idol. This kind of sacrifice they consider the best and most acceptable by all. (*RH Major, pp. 6, 28*)

ABDUL RAZZAQ

An envoy from the Persian court of Shahrukh in Herat, Abdul Razzaq travelled through
South India in 1442-44, making an official visit to Vijayanagara in 1443 during the reign of
Devaraya II.

The city of Bidjnagar [Vijayanagara] is such that the pupil of the eye has never seen a place like it, and the ear of intelligence has never been informed that there existed anything to equal it in the world. It is built in such a manner that seven citadels and the same number of walls enclose each other. Around the first citadel are stones of the height of a man, one half of which is sunk in

the ground while the other half rises above it. These are fixed one beside the other in such a manner that no horse or foot soldier could boldly or with ease approach the citadel.

The fortress is in the form of a circle, situated on the summit of a hill, and is made of stone and mortar, with strong gates where guards are always posted, who are very diligent in the collection of taxes.

The seventh fortress is placed in the centre of the others, and in that is situated the palace of the king. From the northern gate of the outer fortress to the southern is a distance of two statute parasangs, and the same with respect to the distance between the eastern and western gates. Between the first, second and third walls, there are cultivated fields, gardens and houses. From the third to the seventh fortress, shops and bazars are closely crowded together. By the palace of the king there are four bazars, situated opposite to one another. That which lies to the north is the imperial palace or abode of the Rai [Raya]. At the head of each bazar, there is a lofty arcade and magnificent gallery, but the palace of the king is loftier than all of them. The bazars are very broad and long [with flower sellers and jewellers].

In this charming area, in which the palace of the king is contained, there are many rivulets and streams flowing through channels of cut stone, polished and even. On the right hand of the palace the Sultan [Raya] there is the diwan-khane, or minister's office, which is extremely large, and presents the appearance of a chihul-sutun, or forty-pillared hall; and in front of it there runs a raised gallery, higher than the stature of a man, thirty yards long and six broad, where the records are kept and the scribes are seated.

In the middle of the pillared hall, a eunuch, called a Danaik, sits alone upon a raised platform, and presides over the administration; and below it the mace-bearers stand, drawn up in a row on each side. When the Danaik leaves the chamber, several coloured umbrellas are borne before him, and trumpets are sounded. Before he reaches the king he has to pass through seven gates, at which porters are seated, and as the Danaik arrives at each door an umbrella [-bearer] is left behind, so that on reaching the seventh gate the Danaik enters alone. His residence is behind the palace of the king.

On the left of the palace there is the mint. In the king's treasury there are chambers, with excavations in them, filled with molten gold, forming one mass.

Opposite the minister's palace are the elephant sheds. The large [elephants] are specifically reserved for the palace. Between the first and second enceintes of the city, and between the northern and western faces, the breeding of elephants takes place. Each [elephant] has a separate stall; the walls are very strong and high. The chains on the necks and backs of elephants are firmly attached to the beams above.

Opposite the mint is the office of the Prefect of the City. Behind the mint there is a sort of bazaar, which is more than 300 yards long and 20 broad. On two sides of it are houses (khanaha) and forecourts (safhada), and in front of the houses, lofty seats are built of excellent stone, and on each side of the avenue formed by houses there are figures of animals, so well painted as to seem alive. At the doors of these houses the courtesans seat themselves.

[The kings] are fond of displaying their pride, pomp, power, and ploy, in holding every year a stately and magnificent festival, which they call Mahanavami. The king of Bidjanagar directed that his nobles and chiefs should assemble at the royal abode. They brought with them a thousand elephants [and] were assembled on a broad plain [where] were raised enchanting pavilions from two to five stages high painted [with] all kinds of figures. Some of these pavilions were so constructed, that they revolved.

In front of the plain, a pillared edifice was constructed of nine stories in height, ornamented with exceeding beauty. Between this palace and the pavilions there was an open space beautifully laid out, in which singers and storey-tellers exercised their respective arts.

The throne of His Majesty was of prodigious size, made of gold inlaid with beautiful jewels. Before the throne there was placed a cushion. During the three days the king sat on the throne upon this cushion. The whole roof and walls of the apartment were covered with plates of gold inlaid with jewels. Each of these plates was about the thickness of the back of a sword, and was firmly fixed with nails of gold. On the first stage, the king's royal seat was placed. This was formed of gold, and was of great size. (*RH Major, pp. 105-21*)

DUARTE BARBOSA

Arriving in Goa together with the first Portuguese fleet in 1501, Barbosa made the journey to Vijayanagara soon after. His account mentions the king of Narsyngua, who is probably Vira Narasimha Tuluva.

Bisnagua [Vijayanagara] is fenced with strong ramparts and by a river as well, on the further side of a great chain of mountains. It stands on a very level plain. Here always dwells the king of Narsyngua, who is a Heathen and is called Rayen [Raya], and here he has great and fair palaces, in which he always lodges, with many enclosed courts and great houses very well built, and within them are wide open spaces, with water-tanks in great numbers, in which is reared an abundance of fish. He also has gardens full of trees and sweet-scented herbs. In the city as well there are palaces of the same fashion, wherein dwell the great Lords and Governours thereof.

The other houses are thatched, but nonetheless are very well built and arranged according to occupations, in long streets with many open places. And the folk here are ever in such numbers that the streets and places cannot contain them. There is great traffic and an endless number of merchants and wealthy men, as well among the natives of the city who abide therein as among those who come thither from outside, to whom the King allows such freedom that every man may come and go and love according to his own creed, without suffering any annoyance and without enquiry whether he is Christian, Jew, Moor [Muslim] or Heathen [Hindu]. Great equity and justice is observed by all, not only by the rulers, but by the people one to another. Here there is a diamond-mine, whence are obtained many good diamonds; all other precious stones are brought hither for sale from Pegu [Burma] and Ceilam [Ceylon], and from Ormus they bring pearls. These precious stones circulate here more freely than elsewhere, because of the great esteem in which they are held. Here also is used the brocades of poorer quality brought for sale from China and Alexandria, also metals both wrought and unwrought, copper in abundance, quick-silver, vermilion, saffron, rosewater, great store of opium, sanders-wood, aloes-wood, camphor, musk and scented materials. Likewise much pepper is used here, which they bring from Malabar [Kerala] on asses and pack-cattle.

All this merchandize is bought and sold by pardaos [gold coins], which are made in certain towns of this kingdom. Those of this place are perfectly genuine, not one of them has been ever found false, nor is now so found.

The King seldom goes forth from this city; he dwells therein with great luxury and without any trouble, for he passes on all the governance of the realm to his Governours. The natives of this land are Heathen like himself; they are tawny men, nearly white. Their hair is long, straight and black. The men are of good height; the women go very trimly clad; their men wear certain clothes as a girdle below, wound very tightly in many folds, and short white shorts of cotton or silk or coarse brocade, with are gathered between the thighs but open in front; on their heads they carry small turbans, and some wear silk or brocade caps, they wear their rough shoes on their feet. They wear also other large garments thrown over their shoulders like capes, and are accompanied by pages walking behind them with their swords in their hands. The substances with which they are always anointed are these: white sanders [sandal]-wood, aloes, camphor, musk and saffron, all ground fine and kneaded with rosewater. With these they anoint themselves after bathing, and so they are always very highly scented. They wear many rings set with precious stones and many earrings set with fine pearls in their ears. As well as the page armed with a sword, they take also another who holds an umbrella to shade them, and of these some

are made of finely worked silk with many golden tassels, and many precious stones and seed-pearls.

The women wear white garments of very thin cotton, or silk of bright colours, five yards long: one part of which is girt around them below, and the other part they throw over one shoulder and across their breasts in such a way that one arm and shoulder remains uncovered, as with a scarf. They wear leather shoes well embroidered in silk; their heads are uncovered and the hair is tightly gathered into a becoming knot at the top on the top of the head, and in their hair they put many scented flowers. In the side of one of the nostrils they make a small hole, through which they put a fine gold wire with a pearl, sapphire or ruby pendant. They have their ears bored as well, and in them they wear earrings set with many jewels; on their necks they wear necklaces of gold and jewels and very fine coral beads, and bracelets of gold and precious stone and many good coral beads are fitted to their arms. Thus the more part of this people is very wealthy.

They teach their women from childhood to sing, play and dance, and to turn about and take many light steps. These women are very beautiful and very bold. The King and the country-people marry almost in our way, and have a marriage-law; yet they marry several wives, especially the rich who are able to maintain them. The King has in his palace many women of position, daughters of the great lords of the realm, and others as well, some as concubines, and some as handmaids. For this purpose the fairest and most healthy women are sought throughout the kingdom, that they may do him service with cleanliness and neatness, for all the service is carried out by women, and they do all the work inside the gates, and hold all the duties of the household. They are all gathered inside the palaces, where they have in plenty all that they required, and have many good lodgings. They sing and play and offer a thousand other pleasures as well to the King. They bathe daily in the many tanks. The King goes to seem them bathing, and she who pleases him most is sent for to come to his chamber.

The King has a certain house as a hall of governours and officials to hear the correspondence and attend to the administration of the kingdom. He punishes severely those who deserve it, and rewards the good with many honours and thanks. When he finds any great Lord or his relation guilt of any crime, he sends for him, and they come in rich litters borne by their servants, with many led horses and mounted men. On arrival at the palace the king is informed, and orders him to enter, and if he does not give a just excuse for his fault, he chastises him in words as thoroughly as he deserves, and besides this, takes from him half of his revenues.

Thus there are always many palanquins and horse-men at the palace gates. The King of Narsyngua has always more than nine hundred elephants; they are of great size and beauty, and he ever takes them with him for reasons of state as well as for war. He has also upwards of twenty thousand horses. These horses are distributed among the great lords, to whom the king makes them over for maintenance, and they must continually give him accounts of them. In the same way he gives them to other noblemen. To the knights he gives one horse each for his own riding, a groom and a slave-girl for his service, and a monthly allowance, and daily supplies as well for the horse and groom, which they fetch from the great kitchens kept up by the King to feed his elephants and horses. These [kitchens] are in many large houses where are very many great copper cauldrons, and in these are many officials who look after the preparation of the food and others who prepare it.

Horses do not thrive well in this country, and live therein but a short time. Those that are here come from the kingdoms of Ormus and Cambaya, and bring in high prices by reason of the great need for them here. Between both horse and foot the King of Narsyngua has more than a hundred thousand men of war continually in his pay, and five or six thousand women whom also he pays to march in his train, and wheresoever he wishes to make war he distributes them according to the number of men whom he sends forth. These are all unmarried, great musicians, dancers and acrobats, and very quick and nimble at their performances. (*ML Dames, pp. 200-12*)

LUDOVICO DI VARTHEMA

Varthema, an Italian traveller, was at the Vijayanagara court during the reign of Vira Narasimha Tuluva, who ruled the kingdom up to 1509. Varthema's description of the city, published in 1510, was the first to appear in Europe.

The said city of Bisinegar [Vijayanagara] belongs to the King of Narsinga, and is very large and strongly walled. It is situated on the side of a mountain, and is seven miles in circumference. It has a triple circle of walls. It is a great place of merchandise, is extremely fertile, and is endowed with all possible kinds of delicacies. It occupies the most beautiful site, and possesses the best air that was ever seen; with certain very beautiful places for hunting and the same for fowling, so that it appears to me to be a second paradise. The king of this city is a pagan, with all his kingdom, that is to say, idolaters. He is a very powerful king, and keeps up constantly

40,000 horsemen. The said king also possesses 400 elephants and some dromedaries.

This King of Narsinga is the richest king I have ever heard spoken of. The king wears a cap of gold brocade two spans long, and when he goes to war he wears a quilted dress of cotton, and over it he puts another garment full of golden piastres, and having all around it jewels of various kinds. When he rides for his pleasure he is always accompanied by three of four kings, and many other lords, and five or six thousand horses. *(J Winter Jones, pp. 125-29)*

DOMINGO PAES

A Portuguese horse-trader, Paes was at Vijayanagara during the reign of Krishnadevaraya. His richly detailed account of Vijayanagara (c. 1520-22) is by far the most extensive of any foreign visitor to the kingdom.

On the approach to Vijayanagara:
Before you arrive at the city of Bisnaga, you have a very lofty serra [mountain] which has passes by which you enter the city. These are called gates. You must enter by these, for you will have no means of entrance except by them. This range of hills surrounds the city with a circle of twenty-four leagues, and within this range there are others that encircle it closely. Wherever these ranges have any level ground they cross it with a very strong wall, in such a way that the hills remain all closed, except in the places where the roads come through from the gates in the first range, which are the entrance ways to the city. Between all these enclosures are plains and valleys where rice is grown, and there are gardens with many orange-trees, limes, citrons, and

radishes, and other kinds of garden produce. Between these hill-ranges are many lakes by which they irrigate the crops mentioned, and amongst all these ranges there are no forests or patches of brushwood, except very small ones, nor anything that is green. For these hills are the strangest ever seen, they are of a white stone piled one block over another in manner most singular, so that it seems as if they stood in the air and were not connected one with another; and the city is situated in the middle of these hills and entirely surrounded by them.

Now turning to the gates of the first range, I say that at the entrance of the gate where those pass who come from Goa, which is the principal entrance on the western side, this king has made within it a very strong city fortified with walls and towers, and the gates at the entrances very strong, with towers at the gates; these walls are made of strong masonry, and inside very beautiful rows of buildings made after their manner with flat roofs. There live in this many merchants, and it is filled with a large population because the king induces many honourable merchants to go there from his cities, and there is much water in it. Besides this the king made a tank there, which is at the mouth of two hills, so that all the water which comes from either one side or the other collects there. This water is brought from a lake which itself overflows into a little river. The tank has three large pillars handsomely carved with figures; these connect above with certain pipes by which they get water when they have to irrigate their gardens and rice-fields. In order to make this tank the said king broke down a hill which enclosed the ground occupied by the said tank. In the tank I saw so many people at work that there must have been fifteen or twenty thousand men, looking like ants, so that you could not see the ground on which they walked, so many there were; this tank the king portioned out amongst his captains, each of whom had the duty of seeing that the people placed under him did their work, and that the tank was finished and brought to completion.

The tank burst two or three times, and the king asked his Brahmans to consult their idol as to the reason why it burst so often, and the Brahmans said that the idol was displeased, and desired that they should make a sacrifice, and should give him the blood of men and horses and buffaloes; and as soon as the king heard this he forthwith commanded that at the gate of the pagoda the heads of sixty men should be cut off, and of certain horses and buffaloes, which was at once done.

This new city that the king made bears the name of his wife of love [Tirumaladevi-ammana] of whom he made it [modern Hospet], and the said city stands in a plain, and round it the inhabitants make their gardens as the ground suits, each one being separate. In this city the king made a temple with many images. It is a thing very well made. [The city's] houses are of only one floor, with flat roofs and towers. They have pillars, and are all open, with verandahs inside and out, where they can easily put people if they desire, so that they seem like houses belonging to the king. These palaces have an enclosing wall which surrounds them all, and inside there are many rows of houses. Before you enter the place where the king is there are two gates with many guards, who prevent any one from entering except the captains and men who have business there; and between these two gates is a very large court with its verandahs around it, where these captains and other honoured people wait till the king summons them to his presence.

This king is accustomed every day to drink a three-quarter pint of oil before daylight and anoints himself all over with the said oil; he covers his loins with a small cloth, and takes in his arms great weights make of earthenware, and then, taking a sword, he exercises himself with it till he has sweated out all the oil, and then he wrestles with one of his wrestlers. After this labour he mounts a horse and gallops about the plain in one direction and another till dawn, for he does all this before daybreak. Then he goes to wash himself; and after he is washed he goes to where his pagoda is inside the palace, and makes his orisons and ceremonies, according to custom. Thence he goes to a building made in the shape of a porch without walls, which has many pillars hung with cloths right up to the top, and with the walls handsomely painted; it has on each side two figures of women very well made. In such a building he despatches his work with those men who bear office in his kingdom, and govern his cities, and his favourites talk with them. After the king has talked with these men on subjects pleasing to him he bids enter the lord and captains who wait at the gate, and these at once enter to make their salaam to him. The salaam, which is the greatest courtesy that exists among them, is that they put their hands joined together above their head as high as they can. Every day they go to make the salaam to the king.

You must know that from it [Bisnaga] to the new city [Hospet] goes a street as wide as a place of tourney, with both sides lined thoughout with rows of houses and shops where they sell everything; and all along this road are many trees that the king commanded to be planted, so as to afford shade to those that pass along. On this road he commanded to be erected a very beautiful temple of stone, and there are other pagodas that the captains and great lords caused to be erected.

On walls, gates, streets and markets:
So that, returning to the city of Bisnaga, you must know that before you arrive at the city gates there is a gate with a wall that encloses all the other enclosures of the city, and this wall is a very strong one and of massive stonework; but at the present time it is injured in some places. They do not fail to have citadels in it. The wall has a moat of water in some places, and in the parts where it was constructed on low ground. And there is, separate from it, yet another

[defence] made in the following manner. Certain pointed stones of great height are fixed in the ground as high as a man's breast. This wall rises in all the low ground till it reaches some hill or rocky land. From this first circuit until you enter the city there is a great distance, in which are fields in which they sow rice and have many gardens and much water, which water comes from two lakes. The water passes through this first line of walls, and there is much water in the lakes because of springs; and here there are orchards and a little grove of palms, and many houses.

Returning, then, to the first gate of the city, before you arrive at it you pass a little piece of water and then you arrive at the wall, which is very strong, all of stonework, and it makes a bend before you arrive at the gate; and at the entrance of this gate are two towers, one on each side, which makes it very strong. It is large and beautiful. As soon as you pass inside there are two little temples; one of them has an enclosing wall with many trees, while the whole of the other consists of buildings; and this wall of the first gate encircles the whole city. Then going forward you have another gate with another line of wall, and it also encircles the city inside the first, and from here to the king's palace is all streets and rows of houses, very beautiful, and houses of captains and other rich and honourable men; you will see rows of houses with many figures and decorations pleasing to look at. Going along the principal street, you have one of the chief gateways, which issues from a great open space in front of the king's palace; opposite this is another which passes along to the other side of the city; and across this open space pass all the carts and conveyances carrying stores and everything else, and because it is in the middle of the city it cannot but be useful.

This palace of the king is surrounded by a very strong wall like some of the others, and encloses a greater space tan all the castle of Lisbon.

Still going forward, passing to the other gate you see two temples connected with it, one on each side, and at the door of one of these they kill every day many sheep. Of their blood they make sacrifices to the idol that is in the temple. There is present at the slaughter of these beasts a jogi [priest] who has charge of the temple. Close to these pagodas is a triumphal car covered with carved work and images, and on one day in each year during the festival they drag this through the city in such streets at it can traverse. It is large and cannot turn corners.

Going forward, you have a broad and beautiful street, full of rows of fine houses and streets of the sort I have described, and it is to be understood that the houses belong to men rich enough to afford such. In this street live many merchants, and there you will find all sorts of rubies, and diamonds, and emeralds, and pearls, and seed-pearls, and cloths, and every other sort of thing there is on earth and that you may wish to buy. Then you have there every evening a fair where they sell many common horses and nags, and also many citrons, and limes, and oranges and grapes, and every other kind of garden stuff, and wood; you have all in this street. At the end of it you have another gate with its wall, which wall goes to meet the wall of the second gate of which I have spoken, in such sort that this city has three fortress, with another which is the king's palace. Then when this gate is passed you have another street where there are many

craftsmen, and they sell many things; and in this street there are two small temples. There are temples in every street, for these appertain to institutions like confraternities of all the craftsmen and merchants; but the principal and greatest pagodas are outside the city. On every Friday you have a fair there, with many pigs and fowls and dried fish from the sea; and in like manner a fair is held every day in different parts of the city. At the end of this street is the Moorish [Muslim] quarter, which is at the very end of the city, and of these Moors there are many who are natives of the country and who are paid by the king and belong to his guard. In this city you will find men belonging to every nation and people, because of the great trade which it has, and the many precious stones there, principally diamonds.

The size of the city I do not write here, because it cannot all be seen from any one spot, but I climbed a hill whence I could see a great part of it. What I saw from thence seemed to me as large as Rome, and very beautiful to the sight; there are many groves of trees within, in the gardens of the houses, and many conduits of water which flow into the midst of it, and in places there are lakes [tanks]; and the king has close to his palace a palm-grove and other rich-bearing fruit-trees. Below the Moorish quarter is a little river, and on this side are many orchards and gardens with many fruit-trees, for the most part mangoes and areca-palms and jack-trees, and also many lime and orange trees, growing so closely one to another that it appears like a thick forest; and there are also white grapes. All the water which is in the city comes from the two tanks of which I have spoken, outside the first enclosing wall.

The people in this city are countless in number, so much so that I do not wish to write it down for fear that it should be thought fabulous; but I declare that no troops, horses or foot, could break their way through any street or lane, so great are the numbers of the people and elephants.

This is the best provided city in the world, and is stocked with provisions such as rice, wheat, grains, Indian-corn, and a certain amount of barley and beans, grams, pulses, horse-gram, and many other seeds which grow in this country which are the food of the people, and there is a large store of these and very cheap. The streets and markets are full of laden oxen without count, so that you cannot get along for them. There is much poultry. In this country there are many partridges. And of these you will find the markets full; as also of quails, and hares, and of all kinds of wild fowl. All these birds and game animals they sell alive. Then the sheep that they kill every day are countless, one could not number them, for in every street there are men who will sell you mutton. Then to see the many loads of lines that come each day, and also loads of sweet and sour oranges, and wild brinjals [egg plant], and other garden stuff in such abundance as to stupefy one. For the state of this city is not like that of other cities, which often fail of supplies and provisions, for in this one everything abounds.

On the north side of the city is a very great river with much water, in which are many fish, which fish are very unwholesome. Now as to the places on the bank of this river. There is a city built there which they call Sengumdym [Anegondi] and they say that of old it was the capital of the kingdom, but there do live in it few people. People cross to this place by boats which are round like baskets; inside they are made of cane, and outside are covered with leather; they are able to carry fifteen or twenty persons, and even horses and oxen can cross them if necessary, but for the most part these animals swim across. Men row them with a sort of paddle, and the boats are always turning round.

On the temples:

Outside the city walls on the north there are three very beautiful pagodas, one of which is called Vitella [Vitthala]; the other is called Aoperadianar [Virupaksha?], and this is the one which they hold in most veneration, and to which they make great pilgrimages. In this pagoda, opposite to its principal gate which is to the east, there is a very beautiful street of very beautiful houses with balconies and arcades, in which are sheltered the pilgrims that come to it, and there are also houses for the lodging of the upper classes; the king has a palace in the same street, in which he resides when he visits this pagoda. The gate has a very lofty tower all covered with rows of men and women and hunting scenes and many other representations, and as the tower goes narrowing upwards towards the top so the images diminish in size. Passing this first gate, you come at once into a large courtyard with another gate of the same sort as the first, except that it is rather smaller throughout; and passing this second gate, there is a large court with verandahs all round on pillars of stone, and in the middle of this court is the house of the idol.

Opposite the principal gate stand four columns, two gilded and the other two copper. That which stands nearest the gate of the temple was given by King Crisnarao who now reigns here, and the others by his predecessors. All the outer side of the gate of the temple up to the roof is covered with copper and gilded, and on each side of the roof on the top are certain great animals that look like tigers, all gilt. As soon as you enter this idol-shrine, you perceive from pillar to pillars on which is supported many little holes in which stand oil lamps, which burn, so they tell me, every night, and they will be in number two thousand five hundred or three thousand lights. Before you get to it there are three doors; the shrine is vaulted and dark without any light from the sky; it is always lit with candles. At the first gate are doorkeepers who never allow any one to enter except the Brahmans that have charge of it, and I, because I gave something to them, was allowed to enter. The principal idol is a round stone without any shape [linga]; they have great devotion of it. This building outside is all covered with copper gilt. At the back of the temple outside, there is a small idol of white alabaster with six arms; in one it has a sword, and in the others sacred emblems; and it has below its feet a buffalo.

Whenever the festival of any of these temples occurs they drag along certain triumphal cars which run on wheels, and with it go dancing-girls and other women with music to the temple, (conducting) the idol along the said street with much pomp.

On the Mahanavami festival:
When the time of the principal festival arrives the king comes from the new city to this city of Bisnaga, since it is the capital of the kingdom and it is the custom there to make their feasts and to assemble. For these feasts are summoned all the dancing-women of the kingdom, in order that they

should be present; and also the captains and kings and great lords with all their retinues.

These feasts begin on the 12th September [1520], and they last nine days, and take place at the king's palace. The palace is on this fashion: it has a gate opening onto to the open space of which I have spoken, and over this gate is a tower of some height, made like the others with its verandahs; outside these gates begins the wall which I have said encircled the palace. At the gate are many doorkeepers with leather scourges in their hands, and sticks, and they let no one enter but the captains and chief people, and those about whom they receive orders from the Chief of the Guard. Passing this gate you have an open space, and then you have another gate like the first, also with its doorkeepers and guards; and as soon as you enter inside this you have a large open space, and on one side and the other are low verandahs where are seated the captains and chief people in order to witness the feasts, and on the left side of the north of this open space is a great one-storeyed building; and the rest are like it. This building stands on pillars shaped like elephants and with other figures, and all open in front, and they go up to it by staircases of stone; around it, underneath, is a terrace paved with very good flagstones, where stand some of the people looking at the feast. This house is called the House of Victory, as it was made when the king came back from the war against Oriya [Orissa]. On the right side of the open space were some narrow scaffoldings, made of wood and so lofty that they could be seen over the top of the wall; they were covered at the top with crimson and green velvet and other handsome cloths, and adorned from top to bottom. These scaffoldings are not always kept at that place, but they are specially made for these feasts; there are eleven of them. Against the gates there were two circles in which were the dancing-women, richly arrayed with many jewels of gold and diamonds and many pearls. Opposite the gate which is on the east side of the front of the open space, there are two buildings of the same sort as the House of Victory of which I have spoken; these buildings are served by a kind of staircase of stone beautifully wrought — one is in the middle and the other at the end. This building was all hung with rich cloths, both the walls and ceiling, as well as the supports, and the cloths of the walls were adorned with figures in the manner of embroidery; these buildings have two platforms one above the other, beautifully sculptured, with their sides well made and worked, to which platforms the sons of the king's favourites come for the feasts, and sometimes his eunuchs.

That I may not forget to tell of the streets that are in the palace I here mention them. You must know that inside the palace that I have spoken of is the dwelling of the king and of his wives and of the other women who serve them, who are twelve thousand in number; and they have entrance to these rows of houses so that they can go inside. Between this palace and the House of Victory is a gate which serves as a passage to it. Inside there are thirty-four streets.

Returning to the feasts, you must know that in this House of Victory, the king has a room made of cloth, with its doors closed, where the idol has a shrine; and in the other, in the middle (of the building), is placed a dais opposite the staircase in the middle; on which dais stands a throne of state made thus, — it is four-sided, and flat, with a round top, and a hollow in the middle for the seat. As regards to the woodwork of it, you must know that it is all covered with silk cloths, and has lions all of gold, and in the spaces between the cloths it has plates of gold with many rubies and seed-pearls, and pearls underneath; and round the sides it is all full of golden images of personages, and upon these is much work in gold, with many precious stones. In this chair is placed an idol, also of gold, embowered in roses and flowers. On one side of this chair, on the dais below, stands a head-dress; this also is made in the same manner. On the other side is an anklet for the foot made in the same fashion. In front of all this, at the edge of the dais, resting on a support were some cushions where the king was seated during all these feasts. The feasts commence thus:

You must know that when it is morning, the king comes to this House of Victory, and betakes himself to that room where the idol is with its Brahmans, and he performs his prayers and ceremonies. Outside the house are some of his favourites, and on the square are many dancing-girls dancing. In their verandahs round the square are many captains and chief people who come there in order to see; and on the ground, near the platform of the house, are eleven horses with handsome and well-arranged trappings, and behind them are four beautiful elephants with many adornments. After the king has entered inside he comes out, and with him a Brahman who takes in his hand a basket full of white roses and the king taking three handfuls of these roses, throws them to the horses, and after he has thrown them he takes a basket of perfumes and acts towards them as though he would cense them; and when he has finished doing this he reaches towards the elephants and does the same to them. Then the king goes again to where the idol is, and as soon as he is inside they lift the curtains of the room, which are made like the purdahs of a tent, and the king sits himself where these are, and they lift them all. Thence he witnesses the slaughter of twenty-four buffaloes and a hundred and fifty sheep, with which a sacrifice is made to that idol. When they have finishes the slaughter of these cattle the king goes out and goes to the other large buildings, on the platforms of which is a crowd of Brahmans, and as soon as the king ascends to where they stand they throw to the king ten or twelve roses. Then he passes all along the top of the buildings, and soon as he is at the end he takes the cap from his head, and after placing it on the ground turns back [to the place] where the idol is; here he lies extended on the ground. When he has arisen he betakes himself to the interior of the building, and enters where they say that a little fire as been made, and he throws into the fire a powder made up of many things, namely rubies and pearls and all other kinds of precious stones, and aloes and other sweet-scented things. The he goes back to the place whence he threw the flowers to the horses, and as soon as he is here all the captains and chief people come and make their salaam to him, and some, of they so desire, present some gifts to him. And the king [then] withdraws to the interior of the palace by that gate which I have already mentioned; the courtesans and dancing-girls remain dancing in front of the temple and idol for a long time. This is what is done during the morning of each day of these nine days, with the ceremonies I have mentioned, and each day more splendid (than the last).

Now, returning to the feasts. At three o'clock in the afternoon every one comes to the palace. There go inside only the wrestlers and dancing-women, and the elephants, which go with their trappings and decorations, those that sit on them being armed with shields and javelins, and wearing quilted tunics. As soon as they are inside they range themselves round the arena, each one in his place. Many other people are then at the entrance-gate opposite to the building, namely Brahmans, and the sons of the king's favourites, and their relations; all these are noble youths who serve before the king.

After all this is done and arranged the king goes forth and seats himself on the dais I have mentioned, where is the throne and the other things, and all those that are inside make their salaam to him. As soon as the king is seated in his place he bids to sit with him three or four men who belong to his race, and who are themselves kings and the fathers of his wives.

There the kings sits, dressed in white clothes all covered with (embroidery) of white roses and wearing his jewels, and around him stand his pages with his betel, and his sword, and the other things which are his insignia of state. Many Brahmans stand round the throne on which rests the idol, fanning it with horsetail plumes, coloured, the handles of which are all overlaid with gold; these plumes are tokens of the highest dignity; they also fan the king with them.

As soon as these [nobles and] soldiers have all taken their places the women begin to dance. Who can fitly describe to you the great riches these women carry on their persons? — collars of gold with so many diamonds and rubies and pearls, bracelets also on their arms and on their upper arms, girdles below, and of necessity anklets on their feet.

Then the wrestlers begin their play. There are blows [given] so severe as to break teeth, and put out eyes, and disfigure faces, so much so that here and there men are carried off speechless by their friends; they give one another fine falls too. They have their captains and judges, who are there to put each one on an equal footing in the field, and also to adjust the honours to him who wins.

In all this portion of the day nothing more is done than this wrestling and dancing of women, but as soon as ever the sun is down many torches are lit and some great flambeaux made of cloth; and these are placed about the arena in such a way that the whole is as light as day. As soon as these are all lit up there are introduced many very graceful plays and contrivances, but these do not stop long; they only approach where the king is and then go out. Then there enter others in other fashion, with battles of people on horseback; others come with casting-nets, fishing and capturing the men that are in the arena. When these amusements are ended, they begin to throw up many rockets and many different sorts of fires, also castles that burn and fling out from themselves many bombs and rockets.

When these fireworks are finished, there enter many triumphal cars which belong to the captains. Some of the cars appear covered with many rich cloths, having on them many devices of dancing-girls and other human figures. When the cars have

gone out they are immediately followed by many horses covered with trappings and cloths of very fine stuff of the king's colours with many roses and flowers on their heads and necks, with their bridles all gilded; and in front of these horses goes a horse with two state-umbrellas of the king. In front of this horse goes another caracoling and prancing, as do all horses here, being trained in that art.

These horses pass twice around the arena and place themselves in the middle of the arena in five or six lines, one before the other, and the king's horses in front of them, all facing the king. As soon as they are arranged in this way and are all quiet there goes out from inside the palace a Brahman, the highest in rank of those about the king, and two others with him, and this chief Brahman carries in his hands a bowl with a coconut and some rice and flowers, while the others carry a pot of water; and they pass round by the back of the horses.

After this is over you will see issuing from inside twenty-five or thirty female doorkeepers, with canes in their hands and whips on their shoulders; and then close to these come many eunuchs, and after these eunuchs come many women playing many trumpets and drums and pipes and viols, and many other kinds of music, and behind these women will come some twenty women-porters, with canes in their hands all covered with silver, and close to them come women clothes in the following manner. They have very rich and fine silk cloths; on the head they wear high caps which they call collaes [kuliye], and on these caps they wear flowers made of large pearls; collars on the neck with jewels of gold very richly set with many emeralds and diamonds and rubies; and besides this many strings of pearls, and others for shoulder-belts. They carry in their hands vessels of gold each as large as a small casket of water. The come in regular order one before the other, in all perhaps sixty women fair and young, from sixteen to twenty years of age. Who is he that could tell of the costliness and the value of what each of these women carries on her person? So great is the weight of the bracelets and gold and jewels carried by them that many of them cannot support them, and women accompany them assisting them by supporting their arms. In this manner and in this array they proceed three times round the horses, and at the end retire into the palace.

When these women retire the horses also go, and then come the elephants, and after making their salaam they too retire. As soon as they are gone, the king retires by a small door which is at the end of the building. Then the Brahmans go and take an idol and carry it to the House of Victory, where is the room of cloth that I have spoken of; and the king at once comes from within, and goes to where the idol is, and offers his prayers and performs his ceremonies. The king [then] retires, and goes to his supper; for he fasts all these nine days, and they eat nothing until all is finished, and their hour for food is midnight.

On the review of the troops:
In this way are celebrated these festivals of nine days. When these days of festivals are past, the king holds a review of all his forces, and the review is thus arranged. The king commanded to pitch his tent of Mecca [Turkish] velvet a full league from the city, at a place already fixed for that purpose; and in this tent they place the idol in honour of which all these festivals are celebrated.

From this tent to the king's palace the captains range themselves with their troops and array, each one in his place according to his rank in the king's household. Those on foot stood in front of those on horses, and the elephants behind the horses.

Now I should like to describe to you how they were armed, and their decorations. The cavalry were mounted on horses fully caparisoned, and on their foreheads plates, some of silver but most of them gilded, with fringes of twisted silk of all colours; others had trappings of Mecca velvet; others had them of other silks, such as satins and damask, and others of brocade from China and Persia.

The horsemen were dressed in quilted tunics, also of brocade and velvet and every kind of silk. Their headpieces are in the manner of helmets with borders covering the neck, and each has its piece to protect the face. They wear on the neck gorgets all gilded, others made of silk with plates of gold and silver. At the waists they have swords and small battle-axes, and in their hands javelins with the shafts covered with gold and silver. All have their umbrellas of state made of embroidered velvet and damask. They wave many (standards with) white and coloured [horse-] tails, and hold them in much esteem. The elephants in the same way are covered with caparison[s] of velvet and gold with fringes, and rich cloths of many colours, and with bells so that the earth resounds; and on their heads are painted faces of giants and other kinds of great beasts. On the back of each one of them are three or four men, armed with shields and javelins. Then, turning to the troops on foot, there are so many that they surround all the valleys and hills in a way in which nothing in the world can compare:

shield-men with their shields, with many flowers of gold and silver on them, others with figures of tigers and other great beasts. Of the archers, I must tell you that they have bows plated with gold and silver; daggers at their waists and battle-axes, with the shafts and ends of gold and silver; they you see the musqeteers with their musquets and blunderbusses and their thick tunics. Then the Moors — one must not forget them — for they were there also in the review with their shields, javelins, and Turkish bows, with many bombs and spears and fire-missiles.

The king leaves his palace riding on the horse of which I have already told you, clothed in the many rich white cloths I have mentioned, with two umbrellas of state all gilded and covered with crimson velvet, and with the jewels and adornments which they keep for the purposes of wearing at such times. Then to see the grandeur of the nobles and men of rank, I cannot possibly describe it all, nor should I believed if I tried to do so; then to see the horses and the armour that they wear, you would seem then so covered with metal plates that I have no words to express what I saw.

There went in front of the king many elephants with their coverings and ornaments, as I have said; the king had before him some twenty horses fully caparisoned and saddled with embroideries of gold and precious stones, that showed off well the grandeur and state of their lord. Close to the king went a cage, and it was gilded and very large; it seemed to me to be made of copper or silver; it was carried by sixteen men, eight on each side, and in it is carried the idol of which I have already spoken. Thus accompanied the king passed along gazing at his soldiers, who gave great

shouts and cries and struck their shields; the horses neighed, the elephants screamed, so that it seemed as if the city would be overturned, the hills and valleys and all the ground trembled with the discharges of arms and musquets; and to see the bombs and fire missiles over the plains, this was indeed wonderful.

In this way it went on till the king arrived at the place where the tent was that I have already mentioned, and he entered this and performed his usual ceremonies and prayers. As soon as the king had finished his ceremonies he again took horse and returned to the city in the same way as he had come, the troops never wearing of their shouting. Truly, I was so carried out with myself that it seemed as if what I saw was a vision, and that I was in a dream.

On the king's palace:
As soon as we had returned to the city of Bisnaga, the governor of that place showed us the palace.

You must know that on entering that gate of which I have spoken, opposite to it there is another of the same kind. Here they bade us stand still, and they counted us how many we were, and as they counted they admitted us one by one to a small courtyard with a smoothly plastered floor, and with very white walls around it. At the end of this courtyard, is another close to it on the left hand, and another which was closed; the door opposite belongs to the king's residence. At the entrance of this door outside are two images painted life like and drawn in their manner, which are these; the one of the right hand is of the father of this king, and the one of the left is of this king. They stand with all their apparel and such raiment as they wear or used to wear when alive. Afterwards we entered a little house which contained what I shall relate.

As soon as you are inside, on the left hand, are two chambers one above the other: the lower one is below the level of the ground, with two little steps which are covered with copped gilded, and from there to the top is all lined with gold, and outside it is dome-shaped. It has a four-sided porch made of cane-work over which is a work of rubies and diamonds and all other kinds of precious stones, and pearls, and above the porch are two pendants of gold; all the precious stonework is heart-shaped, and, interweaved between one and another, is a twist of thick seed-pearl work. In this chamber was a bed which had feet similar to the porch, the cross-bars covered with gold, and there was on it a mattress of black satin; it had all round it a railing of pearls a span wide; on it were two cushions. In this house there is a room with pillars of carved stone; this room is all of ivory, as well the chamber as the walls, from top to bottom, and the pillars of the cross-timbers at the top had roses and flowers of lotuses all of ivory — it is so rich and beautiful that you would hardly find anywhere another such. On this same side is designed in painting all the ways of life of the men who have been here even down to the Portuguese, from which the king's wives can understand the manner in which each one lives in his own country. In this house are two thrones covered with gold, and a cot of silver with its curtains. Here I saw a little slab of green jasper, which is held for a great thing in this house. Close to where this jasper is, there is a little door closed with some padlocks: they told us that inside it there was a treasury of one of the former kings.

As soon as we left this house we entered a courtyard as large as an arena for beast-fights, very well plastered, and almost in the middle are some pillars of wood, with a cross beam at the top all covered with copper gilt, and in the middle four chains of silver links with hooks; this serves for a swing for the wives of the king. At the entrance of this courtyard on the right hand we mounted four or five steps and entered some beautiful houses made in the way I have already told you — for their houses are single-storeyed houses with flat roofs on top. There is a building there built on many pillars, which are of stone-work, and so also is all the work of the roof, with all the rest of wood, and all the pillars are gilded so that they seem as if covered with gold.

Then at the entrance of this building in the middle nave, there is, standing on four pillars, a canopy covered with many figures of dancing-women. You must know that they make no use of this building because it belongs to their idol and to temple. At the end of this is a little closed door where the idol is.

Descending from this building, we entered a corridor in which we saw some things. On entering the corridor was a cot suspended in the air by silver chains. In front of this cot was a chamber where was another cot suspended in the air by chains of gold. Passing this chamber along the corridor in front was [another] chamber which this king commanded to be made; on the outside were figures of women with bows and arrows like amazons. Passing this corridor and mounting up into another which is here, we saw at one end three caldrons of gold, so large that in each one they could cook half a cow. Thence we went up by a little staircase, and entered by a little door into a building which is in this manner. This hall is where the king sends his women to be taught to dance. It is a long hall and not very wide, all of stone sculpture on pillars, which are at a distance of quite an arm's length from the wall. In the supports on top are many great beasts like elephants, and of other shapes; there are also figures of men turned back to back, and other beasts of different sorts. And on the pillars are other images, [arranged] in such a way that I saw this work gradually diminishing in size from pillar to pillar. But the other images seated on the elephants, as well as those on panels, are all dancing women having little drums. The designs of these panels show the positions at the ends of dances in such a way that on each panel there is a dancer in the proper position; this is to teach the women.

At the end of this house on the left hand is a painted recess where the women cling with their hands in order to better stretch and loosen their bodies and legs; there they teach them to make the whole body supple, in order to make their dancing more graceful. At the other end, on the right, in the place where the king places himself to watch them dancing, all the floors and walls where he sits are covered with gold.

They did not show us more than this. The residence of the women no one may see except the eunuchs. From here we returned by the way we had entered to the second gate, and there they again counted us. (R Sewell, pp. 242-90)

FERNAO NUNIZ

Nuniz, a Portuguese horse-trader, was at Vijayanagara (c 1535-37) during the reign of Achyutaraya, who ruled the kingdom till 1542.

On the foundation of the city:

The King going one day a-hunting, as was often his wont, to a mountain on the other side of the river of Nagumdym [Anegondi], where now the city of Bisnaga [Vijayanagara], — which at that time was a desert place in which much hunting took place, and which the King had reserved for his own amusement, —- being in it with his dogs and appurtenances of the chase, a hare rose up before him, which, instead of fleeing from the dogs, ran towards them and bit them all, so none of them dared go near it for the harm that it did them. And seeing this, the King, astonished at so feeble a thing biting dogs which had already caught for him at tiger and a lion, judged it to be not really a hare but (more likely) a prodigy; and he at once turned back to the city of Nagumdym.

And arriving at the river, he met a hermit who was walking along the bank, a man holy among them, to who he told what had happened concerning the hare. And the hermit, wondering at it, said to the King that he should turn back with him and show him the place where so marvellous a thing had happened; and being there, the hermit said that the King ought in that place to erect houses in which he could dwell, and build a city, for the prodigy meant that this would be the strongest city in the world, and that it would never be captured by his enemies, and would be the chief city the kingdom. So the King did, and on that very day began work on his houses, and he enclosed the city round about; and that done he left Nagumdym and soon filled the new city with people. And he gave it the name Vydiajuna [Vidyaranya], for so the hermit called himself who had bidden him construct it; but in the course of time this name has become corrupted, and it is now called Bisnaga. And after the hermit was dead the King raised a very grand temple [to Virupaksha] in honour of him and gave much revenue to it. And ever since, in his memory, the Kings of Bisnaga, on the day when they are raised to be kings, have, in honour of the hermit, to enter this house before they enter their own; and they offer many prayers in it, and celebrate many feasts there every year.

On damming the river:

This King made in the city of Bisnaga many walls and towers and enclosed it anew. Now the city at that time was of no use, there being no water in it by which could be raised gardens and orchards, except the water of the Nagumdym which was far from it, for what water there was in the country was all brackish and allowed nothing to grow; and the King, desiring to increase that city and make it the best in the kingdom, determined to bring to it a very large river which was at a distance of five leagues away, believing that it would cause much profit if brought inside the city. And so he did, damming the river itself with great boulders; and according to story he threw in a stone so great that it alone made the river follow the King's will. It was dragged thither by a number of elephants of which there are many in the kingdom; and the water so brought he carries through such parts of the city as he pleased. This water proved of such use to the city that it increased his

revenue by more than three hundred and fifty thousand pardaos. By means of this water they made round about the city a quantity of gardens and orchards and great groves of trees and vineyards, of which this country has, and many plantations of lemons and oranges and roses, and other trees in which this country bear very good fruit.

On the palace of Achyutaraya:

All the service of this house, with the things they make use of, is of silver and gold, that is to say basins and bowls, stools, ewers, and other vessels of that sort. The bedsteads in which his wives sleep are covered and adorned with silver plates. Every wife has her bed in which she sleeps, and that of the King is plated and lined and has all its legs of gold, its mattress of silk, and its round bolster worked round the ends with large seed pearls. It has four pillows of the same pattern for the feet, and has no other sheet than a silk cloth on top. He always carries with him a mosquito curtain with a frame of silver.

He has five hundred wives and as many less or more as he wants, with whom he sleeps; and all of these burn themselves at his death. When he journeys to any place he takes twenty-five or thirty of his most favourite wives, who go with him, each one in her palanqueen with poles.

In his palace within the gates he is served by women and eunuchs numbering fully five or six hundred; and these wives of the King all have their own officials for their service, each for herself, just as the King has within the gates, but these are all women. The palaces of the king are large and with large rooms; they have cloisters like monasteries, with cells, and in each one is one of his wives, and with each of these ladies is her maid-servant; and when the King retires to rest he passes through these cloisters, and his wives stand at the doors and call him in; but these are not the principal wives, they are the daughters of captains and nobles of the country. Inside the gates of the palace they say that there are over two hundred milch-cows, from the milk of which they make butter for these ladies to eat.

The King has no expense in connection with his food, because the nobles send it to him every day to his house, namely rice and wheat and meat and fowls with all other necessary things. In the kitchen there are some two hundred inferior guards and four over it, and two chief officers of the guard; and those who are captains of the guard of this King are also captains of soldiers; these porters do not go further inside than through four or five doors, because inside of these are none but eunuchs and women.

On the Mahanavami festival:

When [the King] wishes to please his captains, or persons from whom he has received or wishes to receive good service, he gives them scarves of honour for their personal use, which is a great honour; and this he does each year to the captains at the time that they pay him their land-rents. This takes place in the month of September when for nine days they make great feasts. Which feasts are conducted in the following manner.

This first day they put nine castles in a piece of ground which is in front of the palace, which castles are made by the principal captains of the kingdom. They are very lofty and are hung with rich cloths and, and in them are many dancing-girls and also many kinds of contrivances. Besides these

nine every captain is obliged to make each one his castle, and they come to show these to the King. The officers of the city are bound to come with their devices each day at night, and in these nine days they slaughter animals and make sacrifice. The first day they kill nine male buffaloes and nine sheep and nine goats, and thenceforward they kill each day more, always doubling the number; and when they have finished slaying these beasts, there come nine horses and nine elephants of the King, and these come before the King covered with flowers - roses - and with rich trappings. Before them goes the chief Master of the Horse with many attendants, and they make salaam to the King. And when these have finished making their salaam there come from within priests, and they bring rice and other cooked edibles, and water, and fire, and many kinds of scents, and they offer prayers and throw the water over the horses and elephants; and they put chapelets of roses on them. This is done in the presence of the King, who remains seated on a throne of gold and precious stones; he never sits except only once in the year. Whilst this is going on there pass by the King fully a thousand women, dancing and posturing before him. After all the devices that have been prepared have been witnessed all the horses of the King pass by, covered with their silk trappings and with much adornment of gold and precious stones on their heads, and then all the elephants and yokes of oxen in the middle of the arena in front of the palace. After these have been seen there come thirty-six of the most beautiful of the King's wives covered with gold and pearls, and much work of seed-pearls, and in the hands of each a vessel of gold with a lamp

of oil burning in it; and with these women come all the female servants and the other wives of the King, with canes in their hands tipped with gold and with torches burning; and these then retired inside with the King. These women are
so richly bedecked with gold and precious stones that they are hardly able to move.

In this way during these nine days they are compelled to search for all the things which will give pleasure to the King.

The King has a thousand wrestlers for these feasts who wrestle before the King. They have a captain over them, and they do not perform any other service in the Kingdom.

And after these nine days are finished the Rao [King] rides out and goes to hold a review of the troops of his captains, and he goes to a length of two leagues between the armed men. At the end he dismounts and takes a bow in his hand and shoots three arrows, namely one for the Ydallcao [sultan of Bijapur], and another for the King of Cotamuloco [sultan of Golconda],and yet another for the Portuguese; it was his custom to make war on the kingdom lying in the direction where the arrow reached furthest. After this is done the King returns home, and on that day he fasts and with him all the people of the land. Within these nine days the King is paid all the rents that he received from his kingdom.

On royal employees:
This King has continually fifty thousand paid soldiers, amongst whom are six thousand horsemen who belong to the palace guard. He has also twenty thousand spearmen and shield-bearers, and three thousand men to look after the elephants in the stables; he has sixteen hundred grooms who attend to the horses, and has also three hundred horse trainers, and two thousand artificers, namely blacksmiths, masons, and carpenters, and washermen who ash clothes. These are the people he has and pays every day; he gives them their allowance at the gate of the palace. The King every year buys thirteen thousand horses of Ormuz, and country-breds, of which he chooses the best for his own stables, and he gives the rest to his captains.

This King has also within his gates more than four thousand women, all of whom live in the palace; some are dancing-girls, and others are bearers who carry the King's wives on their shoulders, and the King also in the interior of the palace, for the King's houses are large and there are great intervals between one house and another. He also has women who wrestle, and others who are astrologers and soothsayers; and he has women who write all the accounts of expenses that are incurred inside the gates, and others whose duty it is to write all the affairs of the kingdom and compare their books with the writers outside; he has women also for music, who play instruments and sing. Even the wives of the King are well versed in music.

The King has other women beside. He has ten cooks for his personal service, and has others kept for times when he gives banquets; and these ten prepare the food for no one save for the King alone. He has a eunuch for guard at the gate of the kitchen, who never allows any one to enter for fear of poison. It is said that he has judges, as well as bailiffs and watchmen who every night guard the palace, and all these are women. (R Sewell, pp. 299-302, 369-71, 376-83)

CESARE FREDERICI

Cesare Frederici, an Italian traveller, spent seven months at Vijayanagara, two years after it was sacked. His report (1567) confirms that the city was only partly destroyed and that Tirumala of the Aravidu dynasty had attempted to re-establish his capital there. Frederici's chronicles were issued in an English translation as early as 1588.

When the newes came to the cities of the overthrowe in the battel [at Talikota], the wives and children of these three Tyrants [Ramaraya and his brothers], with their lawfull king [Sadashiva] ... fled away ... and the foure kings of the Moores [sultans of Bidar, Bijapur, Golconda and Ahmadnagar] entered the Citie of Bezeneger [Vijayanagara] with great triumph, and there they remained six months, searching under houses and in all places for money and other things that were hidden, and then they departed to their owne kingdomes, because they were not able to maintayne such a kingdome as that was, so farre distant from their own Countrie.

When the kings were departed from Bezenegar, this Temiragio [Tirumala] returned to the Citie, and then beganne to repopulate it.

In the year 1567 for the ill successe that the people of Bezeneger had, in that their Citie was sacked by the foure kings, the king with his Court went to dwell in a Castle eight dayes journey up in the land from Bezeneger, called Penegonde [Penukonda].

The Citie of Bezeneger is not altogether destroyed, yet the houses stand still, but emptie, and there is dwelling in them nothing, as is reported, but Tygers and other wild beasts. (S Purchas, pp. 92-97)

ALEXANDER GREENLAW PHOTOGRAPHS

Modern photographic prints from waxed-paper negatives taken by Colonel Alexander Greenlaw in 1856.

Gateway and mandapa on Hemakuta hill (*above*). Elephant stables (*below*)

Watchtower and compound walls of the zenana enclosure (*above*)

Lotus Mahal (*above*). Principal gopura of the Virupaksha temple complex with gateway in the foreground (*top*)

Pavilion standing in the tank near the Vitthala temple complex (*above*). Yali columns of the free-standing mandapa in the Vitthala temple (*top right*)

148

Free-standing *mandapa* in the Vitthala temple (*above*). Minor shrine of the Hazara Rama temple (*top left*). Interior of the great open mandapa of the Vitthala temple (*top right*)

Mandapa and chariot-like Garuda shrine (tower now demolished) inside the Vitthala temple (*above*). Entrance gopura and column (now fallen) in front of the Vitthala temple (*top*)

Mandapa and entrance *gopura* of the Krishna temple complex (*above*). Entrance to the Hazara Rama temple (*below*). Interior courtyard of the Virupaksha temple complex with the Kanakagiri *gopura* rising over the colonnade (*right*)

GLOSSARY *Restricted to Indian names and terms*

Achyutaraya, Tuluva emperor (1529-42)
alvar, Vaishnava saint
Ananta, cosmic serpent
Anantashayana, Vishnu asleep on Ananta
Anjaneya, name of Hanuman
avatara, incarnation of Vishnu
Bahmanis, 14th-15th century sultans of the Deccan
Bhuvaneshvari, name of Parvati, consort of Shiva
Bukka, Sangama king (1356-77)
bund, dam wall
chhatra, rest-house
Devaraya I, Sangama emperor (1406-22)
Devaraya II, Sangama emperor (1424-46)
dipa-stambha, lamp column
Durga, **Durgadevi**, fierce goddess who empowers kings
Ganesha, popular elephant-headed deity
Garuda, eagle mount of Vishnu
ghat, stepped bathing place; mountainous ridge
gopura, towered entrance gateway
Hanuman, monkey hero in the *Ramayana*
Harihara I, Sangama king (1336-56)
Harihara II, Sangama king (1377-1404)
Hiranyakashipu, demon disembowelled by Narasimha
Hoysalas, 12th-13th century rulers of southern Karnataka
kalasha, pot-shaped finial
Kali, fierce form of Devi
Kama, god of love
Kampila, pre-Vijayanagara period king (1315-27)
Kishkindha, monkey kingdom in the *Ramayana*
Kodandarama, Rama crowned
Krishna, popular incarnation of Vishnu
Kishnadevaraya, Tuluva emperor (1509-29)
kuta, square-to-dome roof form
Lakshmana, brother of Rama in the *Ramayana*
Lakshmi, consort of Vishnu
linga, phallic emblem of Shiva
Mahabharata, epic story of the battle between the Pandavas and Kauravas

Mahanavami, nine-day festival celebrating Durga, held in September-October
Mahishasuramardini, Durga slaying the buffalo demon
mandala, geometric diagram symbolizing cosmic order
mandapa, columned hall
Matanga, sage who curses Vali in the *Ramayana*
matha, Hindu religious establishment
naga, snake
nagakal, snake stone
Nandi, bull mount of Shiva
Narasimha, fierce man-lion incarnation of Vishnu
Narasimha, Saluva emperor (1485-91)
Pampa, **Pampadevi**, local goddess worshipped at Hampi; consort of Virupaksha
pura, urban quarter
Raghunatha, name of Vishnu
Rama, hero of the *Ramayana*; incarnation of Vishnu
Ramanuja, 12th-century Vaishnava saint
Ramaraya, regent of Sadashiva who usurped power
Ramayana, story of Rama
Rashtrakutas, 8th-9th century rulers of northern Karnataka
Ravana, demon vanquished by Rama in the *Ramayana*
Sadashiva, Tuluva emperor (1542-65)
Saluvas, second dynasty of Vijayanagara
Sangamas, first dynasty of Vijayanagara
sati, ritual suicide
Shaiva, pertaining to the cult of Shiva
Shiva, major Hindu cult deity
Sita, wife of Rama
Sugriva, monkey king of Kishkindha, crowned by Lakshmana
tirtha, sacred bathing spot
tirthankara, Jain saint
Tirumangai, one of the *alvars*
Tiruvengalanatha, name of Venkateshvara
Tuluvas, third dynasty of Vijayanagara
Venkateshvara, form of Vishnu
Vaishnava, pertaining to the cult of Vishnu

Vali, monkey king of Kishkindha killed by Rama
Vasantotsava, spring festival held in February-March
Vidyaranya, sage
Virabhadra, fierce warrior form of Shiva
Virashaiva, Shaiva cult founded in the 12th century

Virupaksha, name of Shiva worshipped at Hampi
Vishnu, major Hindu cult deity
Vitthala, form of Krishna
yali, fantastic leonine beast
zenana, women's quarter

SELECT BIBLIOGRAPHY

DALLAPICCOLA, ANNA L & ANILA VERGHESE. *Sculpture at Vijayanagara: Iconography and Style* (Vijayanagara Monograph Series). New Delhi: Manohar, 1998

DALLAPICCOLA, ANNA L, JOHN M FRITZ, GEORGE MICHELL & S RAJASEKHARA. *The Ramachandra Temple at Vijayanagara* (Vijayanagara Monograph Series). New Delhi: Manohar, 1991

DAMES, ML. *The Book of Duarte Barbosa.* Vol. I. London: 1918. Reprinted New Delhi, 1989

DAVISON-JENKINS, DOMINIC. *The Irrigation and Water Supply Systems of Vijayanagara* (Vijayanagara Monograph Series). New Delhi: Manohar, 1997

DEVAKUNJARI, D. *HAMPI.* Reprint New Delhi: Archaeological Survey of India, 1992

DEVARAJ, D & CHANNABASAPPA S PATIL (EDS). *Vijayanagara: Progress of Research.* Reports 1984-91. Mysore: Directorate of Archaeology and Museums

ELLIOT, HM & J DOWSON (EDS). *The History of India as Told by its own Historians.* Vol IV. London: 1872

FILLIOZAT, PIERRE-SYLVAIN & VASUNDHARA FILLIOZAT. *Hampi-Vijayanagar, The Temple of Vithala.* New Delhi: Sitaram Bhartia INSTITUTE OF SCIENTIFIC RESEARCH, 1988

FILLIOZAT, VASUNDHARA (ED). *Vijayanagara, As Seen by Domingo Paes and Fernao Nuniz (16th Century Portuguese Chroniclers) and Others.* New Delhi: National Book Trust, 1999

FRITZ, JOHN M & GEORGE MICHELL. *New Light on Hampi, Recent Research at Vijayanagara.*

Mumbai: Marg, 2001

—. *Hampi: A Story in Stone*, Mumbai: Eminence Designs, 2009.

FRITZ, JOHN M, GEORGE MICHELL & MS NAGARAJA RAO. *Where Kings and Gods Meet: The Royal Centre at Vijayanagara.* Tucson: University of Arizona Press, 1984

GOLLINGS, J, JOHN M FRITZ & GEORGE MICHELL. *City of Victory, Vijayanagara: The Medieval Capital of South India.* New York: Aperture, 1991

JONES, J WINTER. *The Travels of Ludovico di Varthema.* London: 1863

KOTRAIAH, CTM & ANNA L DALLAPICCOLA. *King, Court and Capital: An Anthology of Kannada Literary Sources for the Vijayanagara Period.* New Delhi: Manohar, 2002

LONGHURST, AH. *Hampi Ruins: Described and Illustrated.* Reprint New Delhi: Asian Educational Services, 1995

MAJOR, RH (ED). *"The Travels of Nicolo Conti, in the East".* India in the Fifteenth Century: Being a Collection of Narratives of Voyages to India. London: 1857. Reprint Delhi: 1974

—. *"Narrative of the Journey of Abd-er-Razzak, Ambassador from Shah Rukh".* India in the Fifteenth Century: Being a Collection of Narratives of Voyages to India. London: 1857. Reprint Delhi: 1974

MICHELL, GEORGE. *Vijayanagara: Architectural Inventory of the Urban Core.* 2 volumes. Mysore: Directorate of Archaeology and Museums, 1990

—. *The Vijayanagara Courtly Style: Incorporation and Synthesis in the Royal Architecture of Southern India* (Vijayanagara Monograph Series). New Delhi: Manohar, 1992

— & PHILLIP B WAGONER. *Vijayanagara: Architectural Inventory of the Sacred Centre* (Vijayanagara Monograph Series). 3 volumes. New Delhi: Manohar, 2002

MICHELL, GEORGE, ED., *Vijayanagara: Splendour in Ruins*, Ahmedabad: Mapin, 2008.

MORRISON, KATHLEEN B. *Fields of Victory: Vijayanagara and the Course of Intensification*. Reprint, New Delhi: Munshiram Manoharlal, 2000

NAGARAJA RAO, MS (ED). *Vijayanagara: Progress of Research*. Reports 1979-84. Mysore: Directorate of Archaeology and Museums

—. *Vijayanagara: Through the Eyes of Alexander Greenlaw, 1856, and John Gollings, 1983*. Mysore: Directorate of Archaeology and Museums, 1988

PATIL, CHANNABASAPPA S & VINODA C PATIL. *Inscriptions at Vijayanagara (Hampi)*. Mysore: Directorate of Archaeology and Museums, 1995

PURCHAS, SAMUEL. 'Extracts of Master Caesar Frederick his eighteen yeeres Indian Observations'. *Purchas His Pilgrimes*. Vol. X. Glasgow: 1905

RUBIÉS, J-P. *Travel and Ethnology in the Renaissance: South India Through European Eyes, 1250-1625*. Cambridge: Cambridge University Press, 2000

SETTAR, S. *Hampi: A Medieval Metropolis*. Bangalore: Kala Yatra, 1990

SEWELL, ROBERT. *A Forgotten Empire (Vijayanagar)*. Reprint New Delhi: Asian Educational Services, 2000

STEIN, BURTON. *The New Cambridge History of India I.1, Vijayanagara*. Cambridge: Cambridge University Press, 1989

TOBERT, NATALIE. *Anegondi: Architectural Ethnography of a Royal Village* (Vijayanagara Monograph Series). New Delhi: Manohar, 2000

VERGHESE, ANILA. *Religious Traditions at Vijayanagara: As Revealed Through its Monuments* (Vijayanagara Monograph Series). New Delhi: Manohar, 1995

—. *Archaeology, Art and Religion: New Perspectives on Vijayanagara*. New Delhi: Oxford University Press, 2000

—. *Monumental Legacy, Hampi*. New Delhi: Oxford University Press, 2002

VERGHESE, ANILA AND ANNA L DALLAPICCOLA, EDS., *South India Under Vijayanagara: Art and Archaeology*, New Delhi: Oxford University Press, 2011.

WAGONER, PHILLIP B. *Tidings of the King: A Translation and Ethnohistorical Analysis of the Rayavacakamu*. Honolulu: University of Hawaii Press, 1993

—. 'Sultan Among Hindu Kings: Dress, Titles, and the Islamicization of Hindu Culture at Vijayanagara'. *Journal of Asian Studies*. 55/4, November 1996

NOTES FOR TRAVELLERS

TRANSPORT

Bangalore to Hampi: about 350 km on NH4 and NH13; approximately 6 hrs by car. Bangalore to Hospet (13 km from Hampi, nearest railhead and city to the site): overnight train (almost 12 hrs) in either direction; overnight buses also available. Hyderabad to Hampi: longer distance and worse roads; more than 10 hrs by car. Secunderabad to Hospet: direct overnight train either way.

NOTES FOR TRAVELLERS   155

Goa to Hampi: about 350 km; bad road with too many trucks, 8-9 hrs driving; the daylight train connection, about 8 hrs, four days a week, is more comfortable. In winter, nightly 'deluxe' bus service in both directions. Train connections are also available to Hospet via Guntakal, Andhra Pradesh, through which pass many of the express services linking Mumbai, Chennai and Bangalore. Buses also run north from Hospet to Badami, Bijapur, Sholapur and Pune, as well as to Shimoga, Mangalore and other points in southern Karnataka.

At Hampi: auto rickshaws and public bus for getting around the site; bicycles can be hired on a daily basis from Hampi bazaar.

ENTRANCE TICKETS
Charges are made for entering the *zenana* enclosure, the Vitthala temple complex and the Archaeological Museum Kamalapur. A daily ticket for both costs Rs 5/- for Indian nationals and US$ 5.00 for foreign nationals.

ACCOMMODATION, FOOD & SHOPPING
Two full days are recommended at Hampi, which usually means spending three nights at or near the site.

Hospet: This rapidly expanding mining city offers a full range of hotels. The newly opened Krishna Palace and Royal Orchid Central, Kireeti, are the most comfortable, but the longer established Malligi Tourist Home, with its terrace restaurant, is also recommended. The Priyadarshini and Shanbagh Towers International are other options.

Kamalapura: The Karnataka Tourist Development Corporation managed Mayura Bhuvaneshwari is especially convenient for visiting the ruins. Banks and a post office are located near the bus stand.

.

North bank of the Tungabhadra:
The remotely situated cottages of the Boulders Resort are popular with foreign tourists. The Kishkinda Trust, which sponsors eco-friendly programs in the region, offers tasteful cottages in Anegondi. Younger visitors on a limited budget will discover an abundance of cheap, simple accommodations on the island directly opposite Hampi.

Toranagallu:
Located 30 km east of Hospet and Kamalapura is the Jindal Steel Works (JSW) complex, with its airstrip suitable for private planes. Here in the pleasant, landscaped residential campus is the comfortable Hyatt Hotel, also the Kala Dham cultural centre, with its permanent photographic exhibit of the Hampi site.

FESTIVALS
Most signficant events in the religious calendar at Hampi:

March-April
Celebration of the marriage of Virupaksha and Pampa, marked by a major chariot festival
November-December
The betrothal ceremony, or phalapuja, of Virupaksha and Pampa
January
Mahasankranti, which always falls in the middle of the month
February-March
Shivaratri (in celebration of Shiva); and the Holi festival, which has become popular in recent years with the local people

The Hampi Festival, staged each year in the first week of November by the Karnataka government, presents a three-day cultural programme of music, drama and dance performances. These are held on a specially erected stage at the end of the bazaar street at Hampi, but sometimes also at other venues around the site.

ILLUSTRATIONS *A listing of archival material*

Watercolours by Indian artists in the service of Captain Colin Mackenzie. December 1799. British Library, London
6   Lotus Mahal
7   Inner court of queen's bath
8-9 *Ruins of Beejanuggur. The Rayels Elephant Stables*
51   First map of Vijayanagara
95   Ganagitti Jain temple

Photographs from waxed-paper negatives by Colonel Alexander Greenlaw. 1856. Alkazi Collection of Photography, London
52   Octagonal Pavilion
97   **(bottom)** Talarighat gate
104 Gateway to the Narasimha temple
144 Gateway and *mandapa* on Hemakuta hill 144-145 Elephant stables
145 Watchtower and compound walls of the *zenana* enclosure
146 Lotus Mahal

146-147   Principal *gopura* of the Virupaksha temple complex with gateway in the foreground
147   **(top)** *Yali* columns of the free-standing *mandapa* in the Vitthala temple; **(bottom)** Pavilion standing in the tank near the Vitthala temple complex
148   **(top left)** Minor shrine of Hazara Rama temple; **(top right)** Interior of the great open mandapa of the Vitthala temple; **(bottom)** Free-standing mandapa in the Vitthala temple
149   **(top)** Entrance gopura and column (now fallen) in front of the Vitthala temple; **(bottom)** Mandapa and chariot-like Garuda shrine (tower now demolished) inside the Vitthala temple
150   **(top)** Mandapa and entrance gopura of the Krishna temple complex; **(bottom)** Entrance to the Hazara Rama temple
150-151   Interior courtyard of the Virupaksha temple complex with the Kanakagiri gopura rising over the colonnade

CREDITS

Courtesy ALKAZI COLLECTION OF PHOTOGRAPHY, London 52, 97 *bottom*,104, 144-151
Courtesy ANUJ KUMAR RAWLA, VR Real Technologies, Bangalore 118, 119, 120
By permission of **The British Library**, London 6, 7, 8-9, 51, 95, 158-159
Courtesy **Clare Arni** 14, 15, 31, 32, 33 *bottom*, 37, 44

bottom, 48, 56, 61, 64-65, 84 *bottom*, 85, 90 *top*, 97 top
Courtesy **John M Fritz** 34-35
Courtesy **John M Fritz & George Michell** inner covers, 62, 99, 106,
Courtesy **George Michell** 30, 36, 45, 46, 50, 87 *centre*, 93

INDEX *Page numbers in bold refer to illustrations*

*Vijayanagara mapped for the first time
in 1799 by Captain Colin Mackenzie*

ISBN 978-81-8495-602-3

TEXT
© 2003 John M Fritz & George Michell

PHOTOGRAPHY
© 2003 John Gollings
unless otherwise indicated

PUBLISHED BY
JAICO PUBLISHING HOUSE
A-2, Jash Chambers, 7-A Sir Phirozshah Mehta Road,
Fort, Mumbai 400 001
jaicopub@jaicobooks.com
www.jaicobooks.com

IN ASSOCIATION WITH
Deccan Heritage Foundation
20-22 Bedford Row
London, WC1R 4JS
+44 207 603 3007
www.deccanheritagefoundation.org